ISBN 978-1-333-42064-2
PIBN 10502217

1 MONTH OF
FREE
READING

at
www.ForgottenBooks.com

By purchasing this book you are eligible for one month membership to ForgottenBooks.com, giving you unlimited access to our entire collection of over 1,000,000 titles via our web site and mobile apps.

To claim your free month visit:
www.forgottenbooks.com/free502217

English
Français
Deutsche
Italiano
Español
Português

www.forgottenbooks.com

Mythology Photography **Fiction**
Fishing Christianity **Art** Cooking
Essays Buddhism Freemasonry
Medicine **Biology** Music **Ancient**
Egypt Evolution Carpentry Physics
Dance Geology **Mathematics** Fitness
Shakespeare **Folklore** Yoga Marketing
Confidence Immortality Biographies
Poetry **Psychology** Witchcraft
Electronics Chemistry History **Law**
Accounting **Philosophy** Anthropology
Alchemy Drama Quantum Mechanics
Atheism Sexual Health **Ancient History**
Entrepreneurship Languages Sport
Paleontology Needlework Islam
Metaphysics Investment Archaeology
Parenting Statistics Criminology
Motivational

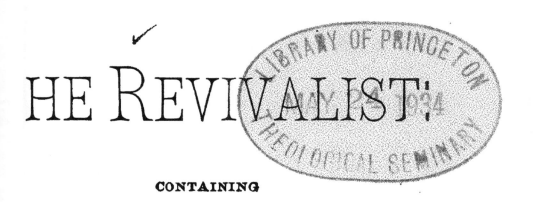

HE REVIVALIST:

CONTAINING

NE HUNDRED CHOICE REVIVAL HYMNS, AND ONE HUNDRED AND TWENTY-FIVE CHORUSES;

DESIGNED FOR USE ON

REVIVAL OCCASIONS.

FIRST EDITION.

NASHVILLE, TENN.:
UMBERLAND PRESBYTERIAN PUBLISHING HOUSE.
1880.

STEREOTYPED AND PRINTED AT THE CUMBERLAND
PRESBYTERIAN PUBLISHING HOUSE,
NASHVILLE, TENN.

PREFACE.

THIS collection was made with special reference to the wants of country churches, on revival occasions. My experience as an evangelist gave me an insight into the wants of those churches, that I am confident this little book will fully supply; for it will give them, at a very small price, just exactly what they need, so that all may sing. It will at the same time, no doubt, be used largely and profitably by town and city congregations.

THE REVIVALIST contains just one hundred revival songs, with a hundred and twenty-five grand old choruses, all sound in doctrine and *extremely devotional* in spirit.

I express my gratitude to the *good brethren* who have so kindly assisted me in this work; and, also, to publishers who gave me permission to use their hymns. I may have used some that I had no right to; if so, it was not intended, and, if notified, I will try to make it satisfactory.

Hoping THE REVIVALIST may contribute largely to the success of revival efforts all over the land, it is most affectionately dedicated to the " Leading Spirits " of the great REVIVAL of 1800.

L. MCWHERTER.

PRINCETON, KY., NOV. 1, 1880.

(3)

O Lord, revive thy work: wilt thou not revive us again, that thy people may rejoice in thee? . . . Sing with the spirit and with the understanding, making melody in your heart to the Lord.—BIBLE.

1   S. M.   WESLEY.

Responsibility.

1 A CHARGE to keep I have,
  A God to glorify;
A never-dying soul to save,
  And fit it for the sky.

2 To serve the present age,
  My calling to fulfil;
O may it all my powers engage,
  To do my Master's will.

3 Arm me with jealous care,
  As in thy sight to live;
And O, thy servant, Lord, prepare,
  A strict account to give.

4 Help me to watch and pray,
  And on thyself rely,
Assured, if I my trust betray,
  I shall forever die.

CHORUS.

(To Jesus My All.)

Jesus my all to heaven is gone,
  And we'll all shout together in that morning;
He whom I fix my hopes upon,
  And we'll all shout together in that morning;
In that morning, in that morning, my Lord,
  And we'll all shout together in that morning.

(5)

2   **C. M.**   **WATTS.**

Sufferings of Christ.

1 ALAS! and did my Saviour bleed?
And did my Sovereign die?
Would he devote that sacred head
For such a worm as I?

CHORUS.

O, how I love Jesus,
O, how I love Jesus,
O, how I love Jesus,
Because he first loved me.
How can I forget thee,
How can I forget thee,
How can I forget thee,
Dear Lord, remember me.

2 Well might the sun in darkness hide,
And shut his glories in,
When Christ, the mighty Saviour died
For man, the creature's sin.

3 Thus might I hide my blushing face
While his dear cross appears;
Dissolve my heart in thankfulness,
And melt my eyes to tears.

4 But drops of grief can ne'er repay
The debt of love I owe;
Here, Lord, I give myself away,
'Tis all that I can do.

3   C. M.   WATTS.

The Christian Soldier.

1 AM I a soldier of the cross,
A follower of the Lamb?
And shall I fear to own his cause,
Or blush to speak his name?

CHORUS.

We will stand the storms,
We will anchor by and by, by and by,
We will stand the storms,
We'll anchor by and by.

2 Are there no foes for me to face?
Must I not stem the flood?
Is this vile world a friend to grace,
To help me on to God?

3 Sure I must fight, if I would reign;
Increase my courage, Lord:
I'll bear the toil, endure the pain,
Supported by thy word.

4 Thy saints in all this glorious war
Shall conquer, though they die;
They see the triumph from afar,
And seize it with their eye.

5 When that illustrious day shall rise,
And all thy armies shine
In robes of victory through the skies,
The glory shall be thine.

4   C. M.   NEWTON.

Amazing Grace.

1 AMAZING grace—how sweet the sound—
  That saved a wretch like me!
I once was lost, but now am found;
  Was blind, but now I see.

CHORUS.

O, never mind the scoffs nor the frowns of the
    world,
For we all have a cross to bear;
It will only make the stars the brighter shine,
When we all get a crown to wear.

2 'Twas grace that taught my heart to fear,
  And grace my fears relieved;
How pricious did that grace appear,
  The hour I first believed!

3 Through many dangers, toils, and snares,
  I have already come:
But grace has brought me safe thus far,
  And grace will lead me home.

4 Yes, when this flesh and heart shall fail,
  And mortal life shall cease,
I shall possess, within the vail,
  A life of joy and peace.

5 And should the earth dissolve like snow,
  The sun forbear to shine;
Still God, who called me here below,
  Will be forever mine.

5

C. M.

Approaching Christ.

1 APPROACH my soul, the mercy-seat,
　Where Jesus answers prayer;
There humbly fall before his feet,
　For none can perish there.

CHORUS.

O, the gospel ship, is a gallant ship;
　A ship both safe and sound;
O, who will sail on the gospel ship,
　For the glorious land she's bound.
Come without money, there is no price,
　No terms could easier be,
For Jesus paid our passage there,
　And we'll have passage free.

2 Thy promise is my only plea,
　With this I venture nigh:
Thou callest burdened souls to thee,
　For such, O Lord, am I.

3 Bowed down beneath a load of sin.
　By Satan sorely prest,
By war without and fears within,
　I come to thee for rest.

4 O wond'rous love, to bleed and die,
　To bear the cross and shame,
That guilty sinners, such as I,
　Might plead thy gracious name!
　　1*

6

L. M.

Expression of Gratitude.

1 AWAKE, my soul, in joyful lays,
And sing thy great Redeemer's praise;
He justly claims a song from thee;
His loving-kindness, O how free!

2 He saw me ruined in the fall,
Yet loved me notwithstanding all;
He saved me from my lost estate;
His loving-kindness, O how great!

3 When trouble, like a gloomy cloud,
Has gathered thick, and thundered loud,
He near my soul has always stood;
His loving-kindness, O how good!

4 Often I feel my sinful heart;
Prone from my Saviour to depart;
But though I oft have him forgot,
His loving-kindness changes not.

5 Soon shall I pass the gloomy vale,
Soon all my mortal powers must fail;
O! may my last expiring breath,
His loving-kindness sing in death!

6 Then let me mount and soar away
To the bright world of endless day;
And sing with rapture and surprise,
His loving-kindness in the skies.

7 6s. WESLEY.

Christ's Intercession.

1 ARISE, my soul, arise,
  Shake off thy guilty fears, ·
The bleeding sacrifice
  In my behalf appears:

CHORUS.

Jesus paid it all,
  All to him I owe;
Sin had left a crimson stain,
  He washed it white as snow.

2 Five bleeding wounds he bears,
  Received on Calvary;
They pour effectual prayers,
  They strongly plead for me:

3 The Father hears him pray,
  His dear anointed one,
He cannot turn away
  The presence of his Son.

4 My God is reconciled,
  His pardoning voice I hear;
He owns me for a child,
  I can no longer fear.

CHORUS.

(*To P. M.*)

Hallelujah to the Lamb, who has purchased
      our pardon,
We'll praise him again when we pass over
  Jordan.

3

8s & 6s.

Sad Gethsemane.

1 BEYOND where Cedron's waters flow,
Behold the suffering Saviour go,
   To sad Gethsemane;
His countenance is all divine,
Yet grief appears in every line.

2 He bows beneath the sins of men,
He cries to God, and cries again,
   In sad Gethsemane;
He lifts his mournful eyes above,
"My Father can this cup remove."

3 With gentle resignation still,
He yielded to his Father's will,
   In sad Gethsemane;
"Behold me here, thy only Son,
And Father, let thy will be done."

4 The Father heard, and angels there,
Sustained the Son of God in prayer,
   In sad Gethsemane;
He drank the dreadful cup of pain,
Then rose to life and joy again.

5 When storms of sorrow round us sweep,
And scenes of anguish make us weep;
   To sad Gethsemane,
We'll look and see the Saviour there,
And humbly bow, like him, in prayer.

CHORUS.

I'm bound for home, for my blissful home,
   The house and the city above;
And all who forsake their sins may come,
   And dwell in that city of love.

L. M. Grigg.

Jesus at the Door.

1 BEHOLD a Stranger at the door!
He gently knocks, has knocked before;
Has waited long—is waiting still;
You treat no other friend so ill.

CHORUS.

O, the Saviour is standing at the door!
O, the Saviour is standing at the door!
Will you let him in? He will cleanse thy sin.
O, the Saviour is standing at the door!

2 O lovely attitude! He stands
With melting heart and bleeding hands·
O matchless kindness! and he shows
This matchless kindness to his foes!

3 But will he prove a Friend indeed?
He will; the very Friend you need;
The Friend of sinners—yes, 'tis He,
With garments dyed on Calvary.

4 Rise, touched with gratitude divine;
Turn out his enemy and thine,
That soul-destroying monster, sin,
And let the heavenly Stranger in.

5 Admit him, ere his anger burn;
His feet departed, ne'er return;
Admit him, or the hour's at hand,
You'll at his door rejected stand.

10

8s & 7s.

An Appeal for Prayer.

1 BRETHREN, we have met to worship
And adore the Lord our God;
Will you pray with all your power,
While we try to preach the word?

CHORUS.

All is vain, unless the Spirit
Of the Holy One come down;
Brethren, pray, and holy manna
Will be shower'd all around.

2 Brethren, see poor sinners round you
Slumbering on the brink of woe;
Death is coming, hell is moving,
Can you bear to let them go?

3 Sisters, will you join and help us,
While we struggle hard with sin;
Will you tell to trembling mourners,
Jesus waits to welcome them?

4 Let us love our God supremely,
Let us love each other too;
Let us love and pray for sinners,
Till our God makes all things new.

CHORUS.
(*To Come Thou Fount.*)

I am happy, I am happy,
And I'm happy in the Lord,
Nor I don't want to stay
Forever here.

11   **C. M.**   W<small>ATTS.</small>

Seeking the Holy Spirit.

1 C<small>OME</small> Holy Spirit, heavenly Dove,
  With all thy quickening powers,
Kindle a flame of sacred love
  In these cold hearts of ours.

2 Look! how we grovel here below,
  Fond of these trifling toys!
Our souls can neither fly nor go
  To reach eternal joys.

3 In vain we tune our formal songs
  In vain we strive to rise;
Hosannas languish on our tongues,
  And our devotion dies.

4 Dear Lord, and shall we ever live
  At this poor, dying rate—
Our love is faint, so cold to thee,
  And thine to us so great?

5 Come, Holy Spirit, heavenly Dove
  With all thy quickening powers;
Come, shed abroad a Saviour's love,
  And that shall kindle ours.

CHORUS.

(*To Jesus My All.*)

O, the Lord has been with us,
And the Lord is still with us,
And he's promised to be with us to the end.

12　　　　　　　C. M.　　　　　　　E. JONES.

Invitation to Sinners.

1 COME, humble sinner, in whose breast
　A thousand thoughts revolve—
Come, with your guilt and fear oppressed,
　And make this last resolve:

2 I'll go to Jesus, though my sin
　Hath like a mountain rose;
I know his courts; I'll enter in,
　Whatever may oppose.

3 Prostrate I'll lie before his throne,
　And there my guilt confess;
I'll tell him I'm a wretch undone
　Without his sovereign grace.

4 I'll to the gracious King approach
　Whose scepter pardon gives;
Perhaps he may command my touch.
　And then the suppliant lives.

5 Perhaps he may admit my plea,
　Perhaps will hear my prayer;
But if I perish, I will pray,
　And perish only there.

6 I can but perish if I go;
　I am resolved to try;
For if I stay away, I know
　I must forever die.

S. M. WATTS.

Christians Rejoicing.

1 COME, we that love the Lord,
  And let our joys be known;
Join in a song of sweet accord,
  And thus surround the throne.

CHORUS.

O, you must be a lover of the Lord,
O, you must be a lover of the Lord,
O, you must be a lover of the Lord,
Or you can't go to heaven when you die.

2 The sorrows of the mind
  Be banished from the place;
Religion never was designed
  To make our pleasures less.

3 Let those refuse to sing
  Who never knew our God;
But children of the heavenly King
  May speak their joys abroad.

4 The hill of Zion yields
  A thousand sacred sweets,
Before we reach the heavenly fields,
  Or walk the golden streets.

5 Then let our songs abound,
  And every tear be dry;
We're marching through Immanuel's
    ground,
  To fairer worlds on high.
    A2

14 8s & 7s. ROBINSON.

Mercies Acknowledged.

1 COME, thou Fount of every blessing,
  Tune my heart to sing thy grace;
Streams of mercy, never ceasing,
  Call for songs of loudest praise.

CHORUS.

I will arise, and go to Jesus,
  He will embrace me in his arms;
In the arms of my dear Saviour,
  O, there are ten thousand charms,

2 Teach me some melodious measure,
  Sung by raptured saints above;
Fill my soul with sacred pleasure,
  While I sing redeeming love.

3 Jesus sought me when a stranger,
  Wandering from the fold of God;
He, to save my soul from danger,
  Interposed his precious blood.

4 O to grace how great a debtor
  Daily I'm constrained to be!
Let thy grace, Lord, like a fetter,
  Bind my wandering heart to thee.

5 Prone to wander, Lord, I feel it;
  Prone to leave the God I love:
Here's my heart, O take and seal it;
  Seal it for thy courts above.

15   8s & 7s.   HART.

Sinners Invited to Jesus.

1 COME, ye sinners, poor and needy,
    Weak and wounded, sick and sore;
Jesus ready stands to save you,
    Full of pity, love, and power:

CHORUS.

Turn to the Lord and seek salvation,
    Sound the praise of His dear name;
Glory, honor, and salvation,
    Christ, the Lord, is come to reign.

2 Now, ye needy, come and welcome;
    God's free bounty glorify:
True belief and true repentance—
    Every grace that brings you nigh.

3 Let not conscience make you linger;
    Nor of fitness fondly dream:
All the fitness He requireth,
    Is to feel your need of Him.

4 Come, ye weary, heavy laden,
    Bruised and mangled by the fall;
If you tarry 'till you're better,
    You will never come at all.

CHORUS.—

Oh, the blood! the precious blood!
    That Jesus shed for me;
Upon the cross, in crimson flood,
    Just now, by faith, I see.

Come to Jesus.

1 COME to Jesus, come to Jesus,
   Come to Jesus just now;
Just now, come to Jesus,
   Come to Jesus, just now.

2 He will save you, etc.

3 He is able, etc.

4 He is willing, etc.

5 He is waiting, etc.

6 He will hear you, etc.

7 He will cleanse you, etc.

8 He'll renew you, etc.

9 He'll forgive you, etc.

0 If you trust Him, etc.

11 He will save you, etc.

CHORUS.

(*To Jesus My All.*)

There's none like lovely Jesus,
   Glory, hallelujah!
There's none like lovely Jesus,
   Glory, hallelujah!

17　　　　　　　**7s.**　　　　　　　Cennick.

The Pilgrim's Song.

1 Children of the heavenly King,
As we journey, let us sing;
Sing our Saviour's worthy praise,
Glorious in His works and ways.

CHORUS.

Let us walk in the light,
Let us walk in the light,
Let us walk in the light,
In the light of God.

2 We are trav'ling home to God,
In the way our fathers trod;
They are happy now, and we
Soon their happiness shall see.

3 O, ye banished seed, be glad!
Christ our Advocate is made;
Us to save, our flesh assumes,
Brother to our souls becomes.

4 Fear not, brethren, joyful stand
On the borders of our land;
Jesus Christ, our Father's Son,
Bids us undismayed go on.

5 Lord! obediently we'll go,
Gladly leaving all below:
Only Thou our leader be,
And we still will follow Thee.

18

C. M.

Keep Praying.

1 Come burdened souls, with all your gilt,
  And all your weight of woe;
There's mercy at a throne of grace,
  Keep praying as you go.

CHORUS.

Keep praying, ever praying,
  Through all our journey below;
To Jesus, to Jesus,
  Keep praying as you go.

2 Behold the precious Lamb who died
  For man, His love to show;
And while you seek the blood-stained cross,
  Keep praying as you go.

3 Young soldiers, gird your armor on,
  And boldly meet the foe;
Let faith direct, and hope inspire,
  Keep praying as you go.

4 Ye pilgrims on the heavenly way,
  Through trials here below,
O, never doubt a Saviour's love;
  Keep praying as you go.

CHORUS.
(*To Come Burdened Souls.*)

It is the hope, the blissful hope,
  Which Jesus' grace has given:
The hope when days and years are past,
  We all shall meet in heaven.

19 S. M. BEDDOME.

Christ In Tears.

1 DID Christ o'er sinners weep?
  And shall our cheeks be dry?
Let floods of penitential grief
  Burst forth from ev'ry eye

2 The Son of God in tears,
  Angels with wonder see!
Be thou astonished, O my soul,
  He shed those tears for thee.

3 He wept, that we might weep:
  Each sin demands a tear;
In heaven alone no sin is found,
  And there's no weeping there.

SONG.—CHORUS.

O, fathers, (mothers, etc.) ar'nt you happy,
And don't you want to go,
To leave this world of sorrow,
And trouble here below?
Lord, I want more religion!
Lord, I want more religion!
Lord, I want more religion,
To help me on to Thee!
Religion makes me happy,
And then I want to go,
To leave this world of sorrow
And trouble here below.

20   C. M.   DODDRIGE.

The Christian's Inquiry.

1 Do not I love thee, O my Lord?
  Behold my heart and see,
And turn each cursed idol out
  That dares to rival thee.

CHORUS.

I want to live a christian here,
  I want to die a shouting;
I want to feel my Saviour near,
  When soul and body's parting.

2 Do not I love thee from my soul?
  Then let me nothing love:
Dead be my heart to every joy,
  When Jesus cannot move.

3 Is not thy name melodious still
  To mine attentive ear?
Doth not each pulse with pleasure bound,
  My Saviour's voice to hear?

4 Hast thou a lamb in all thy flock
  I would disdain to feed?
Hast thou a foe, before whose face
  I fear thy cause to plead?

5 Thou knowest I love thee, dearest Lord,
  But oh! I long to soar
Far from the sphere of mortal joys,
  And learn to love thee more.

21　　　　　　　7s & 6s.

The Mourner's Comforter.

1 DROOPING souls, no longer grieve,
　　Heaven is propitious;
If on Christ you do believe,
　　You shall find him precious.

CHORUS.

　　Jesus' blood has heal'd my wound,
　　　　Oh! the wondrous story;
　　I was lost, but now I'm found—
　　　　Glory! glory! glory!

2 Jesus now is passing by,
　　Calls the mourner to him;
He has died for you and me,
　　Now look up and view him.

3 From his hands, his feet, his side,
　　Runs the healing lotion;
See the rich, consoling tide,
　　Boundless as the ocean.

4 See the living waters move,
　　For the sick and dying;
Now resolve to find his love,
　　Or to perish trying.

5 Streaming mercy, how it flows,
　　Now I know I feel it;
Half has never yet been told,
　　Yet I want to tell it.

2B

22

L. M.

The Land for Me.

1 FAREWELL, farewell to all below,
My Saviour calls and I must go;
I launch my boat upon the sea—
This land is not the land for me.

2 I find the winding path of sin
A rugged road to travel in—
Beyond the chilling waves I see
The land my Saviour bought for me.

3 A few more days, or years at most,
We'll enter on fair Canaan's coast,
The land of Paradise to see,
And that's the land, the land for me.

4 O sinner, why will you not go!
There's room enough for you, I know—
My boat is sound, and passage free,
And there's a better land for thee.

5 Farewell, dear friends, I cannot stay,
The home I seek is far away;
Where Christ is not I cannot be,
That land is not the land for me.

6 There is a land prepared for me,
The price was paid on Calvary;
I have some friends I hope to see,
And that's the land, the land for me.

23   L. M.

The Pilgrim's Farewell.

1 FAREWELL, dear friends, I must be gone,
   I have no home or stay with you;
I'll take my staff and travel on,
   Till I a better world shall view.

CHORUS.

   I'll march to Canaan's land,
      I'll land on Canaan's shore,
   Where pleasures never end,
      And partings are no more.
   Farewell, farewell, farewell,
   My loving friends, farewell!

2 Farewell, my brethren in the Lord,
   To you I'm bound in cords of love;
Yet we believe his gracious words,
   That soon we all shall meet above.

3 Farewell, old soldiers of the cross,
   You've struggled long and hard for heaven
You've counted all things here but dross,
   Fight on, the crown shall soon be given.

4 Farewell, poor careless sinners, too,
   It grieves my heart to leave you here.
Eternal vengeance waits for you,
   O, turn and find salvation near.

CHORUS.
(*To any L. M.*)

O, come, and let us go; let us go, let us go,
O, come, and let us go, where pleasure never
    dies.

24   L. M.   STOWELL.

The Mercy Seat.

1 From every stormy wind that blows,
From every swelling tide of woes,
There is a calm, a sure retreat,
'Tis found beneath the Mercy Seat.

2 There is a place where Jesus sheds
The oil of gladness on our heads;
A place than all besides more sweet—
It is the blood-bought Mercy Seat.

3 There is a scene where spirits blend,
Where friend holds fellowship with friend,
Tho' sundered far—by faith they meet
Around one common Mercy Seat.

4 Ah! whither could we flee for aid,
When tempted, desolate, dismayed—
Or how the host of hell defeat,
Had suffering saints no Mercy Seat.

5 There! there, on eagle wing we soar,
And sin and sense seem all no more,
And heaven comes down our souls to greet,
And glory crowns the Mercy Seat.

6 O, let my hand forget her skill,
My tongue be silent, cold, and still,
This bounding heart forget to beat,
If I forget the Mercy Seat.

25   **11s.**   KIRKHAM.

The Christian's Security.

1 How firm a foundation, ye saints of the Lord,
Is laid for your faith in his excellent word!
What more can he say than to you he hath said?
You, who unto Jesus for refuge have fled.

CHORUS.

I have some friends in glory,
I some time hope to see.
And I've others on their journey,
And they'll pray for me.

2 In every condition, in sickness, in health,
In poverty's vale, or abounding in wealth;
At home and abroad, on the land, on the sea,
"As thy days may demand, shall thy strength
ever be."

3 "Fear not, I am with thee, O be not dismayed,
I, I am thy God, and will still give thee aid;
I'll strengthen thee, help thee, and cause thee
to stand,
Upheld by my righteous, omnipotent hand.

4 Even down to old age, all my people shall
prove,
My sov'reign, eternal, unchangeable love;
And when hoary hairs shall their temples adorn,
Like lambs they shall still in my bosom be
borne.

5 The soul that on Jesus hath leaned for repose,
I will not, I will not desert to his foes!
That soul, tho' all hell should endeavor to shake,
I'll never—no never—no never forsake!"

6s & 9s.

Joy of a Convert.

1 How happy are they
Who their Saviour obey,
And have laid up their treasure above!
Tongue can never express
The sweet comfort and peace,
Of a soul in its earliest love.

2 That sweet comfort was mine
When the favor divine
I had found in the blood of the Lamb.
When at first I believed,
What true joy I received,
What a heaven in Jesus' sweet name ı

3 'Twas a heaven below
My Redeemer to know;
And the angels could do nothing more
Than to fall at his feet,
And the story repeat,   .
And the Lover of sinners adore.

4 Now my remnant of days
Would I spend to his praise,
Who hath died my poor soul to redeem;
Whether many or few,
All my years are his due,
May they all be devoted to him

27   11s & 12s.

Longing for Heaven.

1 I WOULD not live alway; I ask not to stay
Where storm after storm rises dark o'er the way,
The few lurid mornings that dawn on us here,
Are enough for life's woes, full enough for its
    cheer.

CHORUS.

Home, home, sweet, sweet home,
Receive me, dear Saviour, in glory, my home.

2 I would not live alway, thus fetter'd by sin,
Temptation without, and corruption within;
E'en the rapture of pardon is mingled with fears,
And the cup of thanksgiving with penitent tears.

3 I would not live alway; no, welcome the tomb,
Since Jesus has lain there, I dread not its gloom;
Then sweet be my rest, till he bid me arise,
To hail him in triumph descending the skies.

4 Oh! who would live alway, away from his
    God;
Away from yon heaven, that blissful abode?
Where the rivers of pleasure flow o'er the bright
    plains,
And the noontide of glory eternally reigns.

5 Where saints of all ages in harmony meet,
Their Saviour and brethren transported to greet.
While the anthems of rapture unceasingly roll,
And the smile of the Lord is the feast of the
    soul.

28

L. M.

Canaan, My Home.

1 I'M glad that I was born to die,
From grief and woe my soul shall fly;
Bright angels shall convey me home,
Away to the New Jerusalem

CHORUS.

Canaan, sweet Canaan,
I'm bound for the land of Canaan;
Oh! Canaan, it is my happy home,
I'm bound for the land of Canaan.

2 Farewell, vain world, I'm going home,
My Saviour smiles and bids me come;
Sweet angels beckon me away,
To sing God's praise in endless day.

3 When to that blessed world I rise,
And join the anthems in the skies,
This note above the rest shall swell,
My Jesus has done all things well.

4 Then shall I see my blessed God,
And praise him in his bright abode
My theme through all eternity,
Shall glory, glory, glory be.

CHORUS.

(*To any L. M.*)

We'll go on and serve the Lord,
Halle-hallelujah;
We'll go on and serve the Lord,
Glory hallelujah!

29

C. M.

The Re-Union of Saints.

1 IMMORTAL joys await the blest,
  On yon eternal shore;
There happy souls forever rest,
  And sorrows are no more.

CHORUS.

  Oh! that will be joyful, joyful, joyful,
  Oh! that will be joyful!
  To meet to part no more—
  To meet to part no more,
  On that delightful shore;
  At Jesus' feet, we all shall meet,
  Shall meet to part no more.

2 Millions have home to glory gone,
  And have obtained the prize;
Still millions more are pressing on,
  To join them in the skies.

3 Those living armies shall, at last,
  On Zion's mountain meet;
When once the stormy Jordan's past,
  Their union is complete.

4 If friendship in this vale of woe,
  With Christians be so sweet,
What gushing ecstacy shall flow,
  When 'round the throne we meet.
    2*

30 12s & 8s. Mrs. Gates.

Home of the Soul.

1 I WILL sing you a song of that beautiful land,
  The far-away home of the soul,
Where no storms ever beat on the glittering
    strand,
  While the years of eternity roll.

2 O that home of the soul, in my visions and
    dreams
  Its bright jasper walls I can see,
Till I fancy but dimly the vale intervenes
  Between the fair city and me.

3 That unchangeable home is for you and for me,
  Where Jesus of Nazareth stands;
The King of all kingdoms forever is he,
  And he holdeth our crowns in his hands.

4 O how sweet it will be in that beautiful land,
  So free from all sorrow and pain!
With songs on our lips, and with harps in our
    hands,
  To meet one another again.

SONG—CHORUS.

O, carry me to heaven, when I die,
To sing the song of Moses, by and by.
O, fathers, (mothers, etc.) are you ready,
And don't you want to go,
To join that happy company
That's gone on before?
O, yes, I want to go to heaven, when I die,
To sing the song of Moses, by and by.

31 · S. M. Dwight. ·

Love to the Church.

1 I LOVE thy kingdom, Lord,
  The house of thine abode,
The Church our blest Redeemer saved
  With his own precious blood.

2 I love thy Church, O God:
  Her walls before thee stand,
Dear as the apple of thine eye,
  And graven on thy hand.

3 For her my tears shall fall;
  For her my prayers ascend;
To her my cares and toils be given
  Till toils and cares shall end.

4 Beyond my highest joy
  I prize her heavenly ways,
Her sweet communion, solemn vows,
  Her hymns of love and praise.

5 Sure as thy truth shall last,
  To Zion shall be given
The brighest glories earth can yield,
  And brighter bliss of heaven.

CHORUS.

(*To on Jordan's.*)

On the other side of Jordan,
  Hallelujah!
On the other side of Jordan,
  Hallelujah!

P. M. Hunter.

The Christian's Home.

1 In the Christian's home in glory
There remains a land of rest;
There my Saviour's gone before me
To fulfil my soul's request.

CHORUS

There is rest for the weary,
There is rest for the weary,
There is rest for the weary,
There is rest for you;
On the other side of Jordan
In the sweet fields of Eden,
Where the tree of life is blooming,
There is rest for you.

2 He is fitting up my mansion,
Which eternally shall stand;
For my stay shall not be transient
In that holy, happy land.

3 Sing, O sing, ye heirs of glory!
Shout your triumphs as you go;
Zion's gates will open for you, ·
You shall find an entrance through.

CHORUS.

(*To How Firm a Foundation.*)

I am going, I'm going to fly away home,
I am going to a city in the skies.

33   C. M.   Newton.

Subdued by the Cross.

1 In evil long I took delight,
  Unawed by shame or fear;
Till a new object struck my sight,
  And stopped my wild career.

2 I saw one hanging on a tree,
  In agonies and blood,
    Who fixed his languid eyes on me,
  As near his cross I stood.

3 Sure, never to my latest breath
  Can I forget that look;
It seemed to charge me with his death,
  Though not a word he spoke.

4 My conscience felt and owned the guilt,
  And plunged me in despair:
I saw my sins his blood had spilt,
  And helped to nail him there.

5 A second look he gave, which said,
  "I freely all forgive;
This blood is for thy ransom paid;
  I die that thou may'st live."

6 Thus, while his death my sin displays
  In all its blackest hue,
Such is the mystery of grace,
  It seals my pardon too.

34   7s.   McDONALD.

Coming to the Cross.

1 I am coming to the cross,
   I am poor, and weak, and blind;
I am counting all but dross,
   I shall full salvation find.

CHORUS.

   I am trusting, Lord, in thee,
   Blest Lamb of Calvary;
   Humbly at thy cross I bow,
   Save me, Jesus, save me now.

2 Long my heart hath sighed for thee,
   Long has evil reigned within;
Jesus sweetly speaks to me,—
   "I will cleanse you from all sin."

3 Here I give my all to thee,
   Friends, and time, and earthly store;
Soul and body thine to be,—
   Wholly thine for evermore.

4 In thy promises I trust,
   Now I feel the blood applied:
I am prostrate in the dust,
   I with Christ am crucified.

5 Jesus comes! He fills my soul!
   Perfected in him I am;
I am every whit made whole:
   Glory, glory to the Lamb.

35   8s & 7s.   BOWRING.

Glorying in the Cross.

1 IN the cross of Christ I glory,
   Towering o'er the wrecks of time;
All the light of sacred story
   Gathers round its head sublime.

CHORUS.

Round the cross of Christ we'll rally,
   Counting earthly things but dross;
God forbid that we should glory
   Only in the sacred cross.

2 When the woes of life o'ertake me,
   Hopes deceive and fears annoy,
Never shall the cross forsake me:
   Lo! it glows with peace and joy.

3 When the sun of bliss is beaming
   Light and love upon my way,
From the cross the radiance streaming,
   Adds new lustre to the day.

4 Bane and blessing, pain and pleasure,
   By the cross are sanctified;
Peace is there that knows no measure,
   Joys that through all time abide.

5 In the cross of Christ I glory,
   Towering o'er the wrecks of time;
All the light of sacred story
   Gathers round its head sublime.

36

L. M.

A Home in Glory.

1 I LOVE my Saviour, yes I do,
And I'll sing glory, glory;
And all the world may love him too,
And dwell with him in glory.

CHORUS.

O glory! O glory!
There's room enough in Paradise
To have a home in glory.

2 I'm glad that I am born to die,
For I'll sing glory—glory,
And shout his praise above the sky,
And live with him in glory.

3 I have some friends before me gone,
Who now sing glory—glory;
And I'm resolved to follow on,
And meet my friends in glory.

4 If you get there before I do,
And find my friends in glory;
You may tell them I'm coming too,
For I'm on my way to glory.

CHORUS.

[*To I Love My Saviour.*]

And I'll sing hallelujah,
And glory be to God on high;
And I'll sing hallelujah,
There's glory beaming from the sky

37 L. M. J. H. F.

A Home Above.

1 I have a home, a home above,
I have a God, a God of love;
I have a Saviour in the sky,
Who bids me come to him on high.

CHORUS.

A home above, a home above,
Where all is joy, and peace, and love,
A home above, a home above,
Where all is joy and love.

2 There through eternity I'll sing
The praises of my Heavenly King;
Aloud my new-born voice I'll raise
To shout my dear Redeemer's praise.

3 Soon angels bright, with music sweet,
Will greet my weary, wandering feet;
And those from here who've gone before
I'll meet upon that angel shore.

4 I have a place above to rest,
Safe folded to my Saviour's breast;
To dwell forever in his love,
Safe in my home, my home above.

CHORUS.

[*To I Have a Home.*]

Will you go? will you go?
Go to that beautiful land with me?
Will you go? will you go?
Go to that beautiful land?

38   C. M.

Confessing Christ.

1 I'M not ashamed to own my Lord,
   Or to defend his cause,
Maintain the honor of his word,
   The glory of his cross.

2 Jesus, my God! I know his name;
   His name is all my trust;
Nor wlll he put my soul to shame,
   Nor let my hope be lost.

3 Firm as his throne, his promise stands,
   And he can well secure
What I've committed to his hands,
   Till the decisive hour.

4 Then will he own my worthless name,
   Before his Father's face,
And in the New Jerusalem
   Appoint my soul a place.

SONG—CHORUS.

O fathers, (mothers, etc.,) will you go with me?
O fathers will you go?
O fathers will you go with me
To the New Jerusalem?
I am bound for the kingdom,
Lord, I'm bound for the kingdom,
I am bound for the kingdom,
With sweet glory in my soul.

39   L. M.   ELLIOTT.

Just as I Am.

1 JUST as I am, without one plea,
But that thy blood was shed for me,
And that thou bid'st me come to thee,
O Lamb of God, I come! I come!

CHORUS.

I can no longer stay away,
I can no longer stay
Where the gospel sounds so sweetly to me,
I can no longer stay.

2 Just as I am—poor, wretched, blind;
Sight, riches, healing of the mind,
Yea, all I need, in thee to find,
O Lamb of God, I come! I come!

3 Just as I am—thou wilt receive,
Wilt welcome, pardon, cleanse, relieve;
Because thy promise I believe,
O Lamb of God, I come! I come!

4 Just as I am—thy love unknown
Hath broken every barrier down;
Now, to be thine, yea, thine alone,
O Lamb of God, I come! I come!

CHORUS.

[*To Just As I Am.*]

O hinder me not!
For I love to serve the Lord,
And I'll praise him when I die.

40   7s. Double.   MARSH.

Jesus Our Refuge.

1 JESUS, lover of my soul,
  Let me to thy bosom fly,
While the billows near me roll,
  While the tempest still is high:
Hide me, O my Saviour! hide,
  Till the storm of life be past;
Safe into the haven guide,
  O receive my soul at last!

2 Other refuge have I none;
  Hangs my helpless soul on thee:
Leave, O leave me not alone!
  Still support and comfort me:
·All my trust in thee is stayed;
  All my help from thee I bring;
Cover my defence ess head
  With the shadow of thy wing.

3 Thou, O Christ! art all I want:
  More than all in thee I find;
Raise the fa'len, cheer the faint,
  Heal the sick and lead the blind.
Thou of life the fountain art;
  Freely let me take of thee:
Spring thou up within my heart;
  Rise to all eternity.

CHORUS.

[*To Arise My Soul.*]

And can it be that "He loved me,
And gave himself for me?"

41   L. M.   CENNICK.

Christ the Way.

1 JESUS, my all, to heaven is gone,
He whom I fix my hopes upon;
His track I see, and I'll pursue
The narrow way, till him I view.

CHORUS.

I am bound for the Promised Land,
I am bound for the Promised Land;
O, who will come and go with me,
I am bound for the Promised Land.

2 The way the holy prophets went,
The road that leads from banishment,
The King's highway of holiness
I'll go, for all his paths are peace.

3 This is the way I long have sought,
And mourned because I found it not;
Till late I heard my Saviour say,
"Come hither, soul, I am the way."

4 Lo! glad I come, and thou blessed Lamb
Shalt take me to thee as I am;
Nothing but sin have I to give,
Nothing but love shall I receive.

5 Then will I tell to sinners round,
What a dear Saviour I have found;
I'll point to thy redeeming blood,
And say, "Behold the way to God!"

42

C. M.

Jerusalem.

1 JERUSALEM, my happy home,
  Name ever dear to me;
When shall my labors have an end,
  In joy, and peace, and thee?

CHORUS.

  I want to go, I want to go,
  I want to go there too;
  I want to go where Jesus is,
  I want to go there too.

2 When shall these eyes thy heaven-built
    walls,
  And pearly gates behold?
Thy bulwarks with salvation strong,
  And streets of shining gold.

3 O, when, thou city of my God,
  Shall I thy courts ascend,   .
Where congregations ne'er break up,
  And Sabbaths have no end.

4 There happier bowers than Eden's bloom
  Nor sin nor sorrow know;
Bless'd seats! through rude and stormy
    scenes
  I onward press to you.

5 Jerusalem! my happy home!
  My soul still pants for thee;
Then shall my labors have an end,
  When I thy joys shall see.

43 8s & 7s. GRANT.

The Cross Taken.

1 JESUS, I my cross have taken,
  All to leave and follow thee;
Naked, poor, despised, forsaken—
  Thou from hence my all shall be!
Perish, every fond ambition—
  All I've sought, or hoped, or known,
Yet how rich is.my condition—
  God and heaven are all mine own.

2 Let the world despise and leave me,
  They have left my Saviour too;
Human hopes and looks deceive me,
  Thou art not, like them, untrue;
I have called thee Abba Father,
  I have set my heart on thee;
Storms may howl, and clouds may gather,
  All must work for good to me.

3 Soul, then know thy full salvation,
  Rise o'er sin, and fear, and care;
Joy to find in every station,
  Something still to do or bear.
Haste thee on from grace to glory,
  Armed by faith, and winged by prayer;
Heaven's eternal day's before thee,
  God's own hand shall guide thee there

CHORUS.

(*To Jesus My All.*)

We are traveling home to heaven above,
Will you go, will you go?

8s & 7s.

The Gospel Ship.

1 Lo! the gospel ship is sailing,
  Bound for Canaan's peaceful shore;
All who wish to sail for glory,
  Come, and welcome, rich and **poor.**

CHORUS.

Glory! Glory! Hallelujah!
  All her sailors loudly cry;
While the blissful port of glory
  Opens to each faithful eye.

2 Thousands she has safely landed,
  Far beyond this mortal shore;
Thousands still are sailing in her,
  Yet there's room for thousands mor**e.**

3 Richly laden with provisions—
  Want, her sailors never know;
Gospel grace and every blessing
  From her noble Pilot flow.

4 Sails well filled with heavenly breez**es,**
  Swiftly waft the ship along;
All her company rejoicing;
  "Glory!" bursts from every tong**ue.**

5 Do not fear the ship will founder,
  Though the foaming billows roar;
Jesus Christ will safely guide her,
  To her destined, happy shore.

7s. HAMMOND.

Seeking a Preparation of Heart.

1 LORD, we come before thee **now**,
At thy feet we humbly bow;
O, do not our suit disdain:
Shall we seek thee, Lord, in vain?

2 Lord, on thee our souls depend;
In compassion now descend;
Fill our hearts with thy rich grace,
Tune **our** lips to sing thy praise.

3 Grant that all may seek and find
Thee a gracious God, and kind;
Heal the sick, the captive free;
Let us all rejoice in thee.

SONG—CHORUS.

Seek him fathers, (mothers, etc.,) seek him early,
Seek him fathers till you find the Lord;
May I tell him you're a coming,
Trusting in his word?
Been a long time seeking,
But now I've found the Lord.
Glory, glory, glory, glory,
Newly born again;
Been a long time seeking,
But now I've found the Lord.

46 S. M. HEATH.

The Soul Warned.

1 My soul be on thy guard,
    Ten thousand foes arise;
The hosts of sin are pressing hard
    To draw thee from the skies.

2 O watch, and fight, and pray;
    The battle ne'er give o'er;
Renew it boldly every day,
    And help divine implore.

3 Ne'er think the victory won,
    Nor lay thine armor down,
Thy arduous work will not be done
    Till thou obtan thy crown.

SONG—CHORUS.

O, fathers, (mothers, etc.,) will you meet me,
O, fathers, will you meet me,
O, fathers, will you meet me
On Canaan's happy shore?
By the grace of God I'll meet you,
By the grace of God I'll meet you,
By the grace of God I'll meet you
On Canaan's happy shore.
Then we'll shout, and give him glory,
Then we'll shout, and give him glory,
Then we'll shout, and give him glory,
For glory is his own.

47 8s & 7s.

The Shining Shore.

1 My days are gliding swiftly by,
  And I, a pilgrim stranger,
Would not detain them as they fly
  Those hours of toil and danger.

CHORUS.

For O, we stand on Jordan's strand,
  Our friends are passing over;
And just before, the shining shore
  We may almost discover!

2 We'll gird our loins, my brethren dear,
  Our heavenly home discerning;
Our absent Lord the watchword gave,
  Let every lamp be burning.

3 Should coming days be cold and dark,
  We will not yield to sorrow;
Our perfect rest naught can molest,
  There's glory on to-morrow.

4 Let sorrow's rudest tempest blow,
  Each cord on earth to sever:
Our King says come, and there's our home
  Forever, O forever.

CHORUS.

(*To Jesus My All.*)

We're going home, we're going home,
We're going home, to die no more;
To die no more, to die no more,
We're going home, to die no more.

18

C. M.

· *Nearing the Better Land.*

1 My latest sun is sinking fast,
  My race is nearly run;
My strongest trials now are past
  My triumph is begun.

CHORUS.

O come, angel band,
Come, and around me stand;
O bear me away on your snowy wings
To my immortal home.

2 I know I'm nearing the holy ranks,
  Of friends and kindred dear,
For I brush the dew on Jordan's banks,
  The crossing must be near.

3 I've almost gained my heavenly home,
  My spirit loudly sings;
The holy ones, behold, they come!
  I hear the noise of wings.

4 O, bear my longing heart to him
  Who bled and died for me;
Whose blood now cleanses from all sin,
  And gives me victory.

CHORUS.

(*To any L. M.*)

I'll never turn back any more,
No more, no more,
My Lord, no more,
I'll never turn back any more.

49   6s & 7s.

Sweet as Manna.

1 My brethren, I have found,
A land that doth abound
   With food as sweet as manna;
The more I eat, I find,
The more I am inclin'd,
   To sing and shout Hosanna

CHORUS.

My soul now longs to go,
Where I shall fully know
   The glories of my Saviour;
And as I pass along,
I'll sing a Christian song:
   I hope to live forever.

2 Perhaps you think I'm wild,
Or simple as a child—
   I am a child of glory;
I am born from above,
My heart is full of love—
   I long to tell the story.

3 My brethren, can't you say,
That you are on the way—
   Are on your way to glory?
I care not what's your name,
Religion is the same—
   A hope that's full of glory.

50

L. M.

Going Home.

1 My heavenly home is bright and fair,
Nor sin, nor sorrow enters there;
Its glittering towers the sun outshine,
That heavenly mansion shall be mine.

CHORUS.

I am on my journey home,
I am on my journey home,
To the New Jerusalem;
So fare you well, so fare you well,
I'm going home.

2 My Father's house is built on high
Above the arched and starry sky.
When from this earthly prison free,
That heavenly mansion mine shall be.

3 While here a stranger far from home,
Affliction's waves may round me foam,
Be mine the happier lot to own,
A heavenly mansion near the throne.

CHORUS.

(*To My Heavenly Home.*)

Come, let us join our hearts and hands,
All in one band completely;
We're marching through Immanuel's lands,
Where the waters flow so freely;
We're marching through Immanuel's lands,
Where the angels sing so sweetly.

6s & 4s. ADAMS.

Nearer to Thee.

1 NEARER, my God, to thee,
  Nearer to thee;
E'en though it be a cross
  That raiseth me.
Still all my song shall be,
Nearer, my God, to thee,
  Nearer to thee.

2 Though like a wanderer,
  Daylight all gone,
Darkness be over me,
  My rest a stone;
Yet in my dreams I'd be
Nearer, my God, to thee,
  Nearer to thee.

3 There let the way appear
  Steps up to heaven;
All that thou sendest me
  In mercy given;
Angels to beckon me
Nearer, my God, to thee,
  Nearer to thee.

4 Or, if on joyful wing,
  Cleaving the sky,
Sun, moon, and stars forget,
  Upward I fly,
Still all my song shall be,
Nearer, my God, to thee,
  Nearer to thee.

! 52   **C. M.**   **COWPER.**

Walking with God.

1 O FOR a closer walk with God!
 A calm and heavenly frame!
A light to shine upon the road
 That leads me to the Lamb!

CHORUS.

Help me, dear Saviour, thee to own,
 And ever faithful be;
And when thou sittest on thy throne,
 Dear Lord, remember me.

2 What peaceful hours I then enjoyed!
 How sweet their memory still!
But now I find an aching void
 The world can never fill.

3 Return, O holy Dove, return,
 Sweet messenger of rest;
I hate the sins that made thee mourn,
 And drove thee from my breast.

4 The dearest idol I have known,
 What'er that idol be,
Help me to tear it from thy throne,
 And worship only thee.

5 So shall my walk be close with God,
 Calm and serene my frame:
So purer light shall mark the road
 That leads me to the Lamb.

53   8s & 7s.

Glory.

1 O SINNER, come, without delay,
   And seek a home in glory;
The Lord is calling you to-day,
   He pleads for you in glory.

CHORUS.

'O glory! O glory!
There's power in Jesus' dying love,
To bring you home to glory.

2 O turn and live, to you he cries,
   And you shall share my glory;
But if my mercy you despise,
   You can not see my glory.

3 Repent, and give him now your heart,
   He is the Lord of glory;
Confess his name, secure a part,
   When he shall come in glory.

4 Now is your time—no more delay,
   For soon he'll come in glory;
If shut without, in vain you'll pray—
   You've lost all hope of glory.

CHORUS.

Palms of victory, crowns of glory.
Palms of victory you shall bear
Shout, O glory, O glory,
Palms of victory you shall bear.

3*

54   C. M.   STENNETT

Heaven in Prospect.

1 ON Jordan's stormy banks I stand,
   And cast a wishful eye;
To Canaan's fair and happy land,
   Where my possessions lie.

CHORUS.

  O heaven, sweet heaven,
    Dear heaven of the blest;
  How I long to be there,
  In its glories to share,
    And to lean on my Saviour's breast

2 O the transporting, rapturous scene,
   That rises to my sight!
Sweet fields arrayed in living green,
   And rivers of delight.

3 O'er all those wide-extended plains,
   Shines one eternal day;
There God, the Son, forever reigns,
   And scatters night away.

4 When shall I reach that happy place.
   And be forever blest?
When shall I see my Father's face,
   And in his bosom rest?

5 Filled with delight, my raptured soul
   Would here no longer stay;
Though Jordan's waves should round me
    roll.
   I'd fearless launch away.

55

7s & 6s.

Longing to be with Jesus.

1 O WHEN shall I see Jesus,
    And reign with him above,
And from the flowing fountains
    Drink everlasting love.

CHORUS.

    I am on my way to Canaan,
    I am on my way to Canaan,
    I am on my way to Canaan,
    To the New Jerusalem.

2 When shall I be delivered
    From this vain world of sin,
And with my blessed Jesus,
    Drink endless pleasures in ?

3 But now I am a soldier,
    My Captain's gone before,
He's given me my orders,
    And tells me not to fear.

4 Through grace I am determined
    To conquer, though I die;
And then away to Jesus,
    On wings of love I'll fly.

5 Gird on the heavenly armor,
    Of faith, and hope, and love,
And when the battle's ended
    You'll reign with him above.

L. M. DODDRIDGE.

Happy Day.

1 O HAPPY day, that fixed my choice,
On thee, my Saviour and my God!
Well may this glowing heart rejoice,
And tell its raptures all abroad.

CHORUS.

Happy day, happy day,
When Jesus washed my sins away:
He taught me how to watch and pray,
And live rejoicing every day,
Happy day, happy day,
When Jesus washed my sins away.

2 'Tis done, the great transaction's done—
I am my Lord's, and he is mine;
He drew me, and I followed on,
Charmed to confess the voice divine.

3 Now rest, my long-divided heart;
Fixed on this blissful centre, rest;
Nor ever from thy Lord depart,
With him of every good possessed.

4 High heaven, that heard the solemn vow,
That vow renewed shall daily hear,
'Till in life's latest hour I bow,
And bless, in death, a bond so dear.

C. M.   DR. MILLER

Waiting for Jesus.

1 O, LAND of rest, for thee I sigh,
  When will the moment come,
When I shall lay my armor by,
  And dwell in peace at home.

CHORUS.

We'll wait till Jesus comes,
We'll wait till Jesus comes,
We'll wait till Jesus comes,
  And we'll be gathered home.

2 No tranquil joys on earth I know,
  No peaceful sheltering dome,
This world's a wilderness of woe,
  This world is not my home.

3 To Jesus Christ I fled for rest;
  He bade me cease to roam,
And lean for succor on his breast,   .
  And he'd conduct me home.

4 I sought at once my Saviour's side,
  No more my steps shall roam :
With him I'll brave death's chilling tide,
  And reach my heavenly home.

CHORUS.

(*To Jerusalem, My.*)

Home, sweet home, my long sought home ;
My home in heaven above.

Judgment Seat of Christ.

1 O, there will be shouting,
Shouting, shouting, shouting;
O, there will be shouting
At the judgment seat of Christ.
Wives and husbands there shall meet,
Wives and husbands there shall meet,
Wives and husbands there shall meet,
Shall meet to part no more.

2 O, there will be mourning;
Mourning, mourning, mourning,
O, there will be mourning,
At the judgment seat of Christ.
Wives and husbands there shall part,
Wives and husbands there shall part,
Wives and husbands there shall part,
Shall part to meet no more.

3 O, there will be shouting;
Shouting, shouting, shouting,
O, there will be shouting,
At the judgment seat of Christ.
Brothers and sisters there shall meet,
Brothers and sisters there shall meet,
Brothers and sisters there shall meet,
Shall meet to part no more, etc.

P. M.

Rejoicing in Hope.

1 OUR bondage here shall end by and by;
    From Egypt's yoke set free,
    Hail the glorious jubilee,
And to Canaan we'll return by and by.

2 Our deliverer will come by and by,
    And our sorrows have an end
    With our threescore years and ten,
And vast glory crown the day, by and by.

3 Then friends shall meet again who have loved;
    Our embraces shall be sweet
    At our dear Redeemer's feet,
When we meet to part no more, who have
        loved.

4 Then, with all the happy throng, we'll
        rejoice,
    Shouting glory to our King,
    While the vaults of heaven shall ring,
And through all eternity we'll rejoice.

SONG—CHORUS.

O, fare you well; O, fare you well;
    When we get to heaven, we will part no more;
Christians (fathers, etc.,) fare you well, O, fare
        you well;
    For when we get to heaven we'll part no more.
If you get there before I do;
    And when we get to heaven, we'll part no more;
Tell all my friends I m coming too;
    And when we get to heaven, we'll part no more.

30 10s & 9s. PHIL.

Let the Master In.

1 ONCE I heard a sound at my heart's dark door
  And was roused from the slumber of sin;
It was Jesus knocked, he had knocked before
  Now I said, "Blessed Master, come in."

CHORUS.

Then open, open,
  Open, let the Master in;
For the   will be bright with a heavenly
    light;art
When you let the Master in.

2 Then he spread a feast of redeeming love,
  And he made me his own happy guest;
In my joy I thought that the saints above
  Could be hardly more favored or blest.

3 In the holy war with the foes of truth,
  He's my Shield, he my table prepares,
He restores my soul, he renews my youth,
  And gives triumph in answer to prayers.

4 He will feast me still with his presence dear,
  And the love he so freely hath given,
While his promise tells, as I serve him here,
  Of the banquet of glory in heaven.

CHORUS.
(*To Jesus My All.*)

I am bound to live in the service of my Lord,
  I am bound to die in the army;
In the army—in the army of my Lord,
  I am bound to die in the army.

61

L. M.

Pilgrims Bound for Canaan.

1 Pilgrims, we are to Canaan bound,
  Our journey lies along the road;
This wilderness we travel round,
  To reach the city of our God.

CHORUS.

O happy pilgrims, spotless, fair,
What makes your robes so white appear?
Our robes are washed in Jesus' blood,
And we are trav'ling home to God.

2 O blessed land! O happy land!
  When shall we reach thy golden shore?
And one redeemed, unbroken band
  United be forevermore.

3 And if our robes are pure and white,
  May we all reach that blest abode?
O yes, they all shall dwell in light,
  Whose robes are washed in Jesus' blood.

4 We all shall reach that golden shore,
  If here we watch, and fight, and pray;
Straight is the way, and straight the door,
  And none but pilgrims find the way.

CHORUS.

(*To Pilgrims We Are.*)

O, heaven, sweet heaven, when shall I see?
O when shall I get there?
    c2

62   C. M.   WATTS.

Deliverance.

1 PLUNGED in a gulf of dark despair,
  We wretched sinners lay,
Without one cheering beam of hope.
  Or spark of glimm'ring day.

CHORUS.

1 own I'm base, I own I'm vile,
  But mercy's all my plea;
Remember, Lord, thy dying groans,
  And then remember me.

2 With pitying eyes the Prince of grace
  Beheld our helpless grief:
He saw, and (O, amazing love!)
  He ran to our relief.

3 Down from the shining seats above
  With joyful haste he fled,
Entered the grave in mortal flesh,
  And dwelt among the dead.

4 O for this love let rocks and hills
  Their lasting silence break!
And all harmonious human tongues
  Their Saviour's praises speak.

5 Angels, assist our mighty joys,
  Strike all your harps of gold;
But when you raise your highest notes,
  His love can ne'er be told!

63

7s.

Rock of Ages.

1 ROCK of Ages, cleft for me,
Let me hide myself in thee:
Let the water and the blood,
From thy wounded side which flowed
Be of sin the double cure;
Cleanse me from its guilt and power.

2 Not the labor of my hands
Can fulfil the law's demands;
Could my zeal no respite know,
Could my tears forever flow,
All for sin could not atone;
Thou must save, and thou alone.

3 Nothing in my hand I bring,
Simply to thy cross I cling;
Naked, come to thee for dress,
Helpless, look to thee for grace;
Vile, I to the fountain fly,
Wash me, Saviour, or I die.

4 While I draw this fleeting breath,
When my heart-strings break in death,
When I soar to worlds unknown,
See thee on thy judgment-throne,
Rock of Ages, cleft for me,
Let me hide myself in thee.

CHORUS.

Sing Glory, Glory, Glory, Hallelujah,
We'll shout when we meet him in the **air.**

64

Revive thy Work.

1 REVIVE thy work, O Lord,
Now to thy saints appear;
Oh, speak with power to every heart,
And let thy people hear.

CHORUS.

Revive thy work, O Lord,
While here to thee we bow;
Descend, O gracious Lord, descend,
And bless thy people now.

2 Revive thy work, O Lord,
And may thy sacred word,
With precious power to every heart,
In living faith be heard.

3 Revive thy work, O Lord;
Give pentacostal showers,
Be thine the glory, thine alone;
The blessing, Lord, be ours.

4 Revive thy work, O Lord,
And hear our humble cry,
And send with a reviving power,
Thy Spirit from on high.

CHORUS.

Kindest and best of the sons of the morning,
Dawn on our darkness and lend us thine aid;
Star of the east the horizon adorning,
Guide where our infant Redeemer was laid.

65

C. M.

Religion.

1 RELIGION is the chief concern
  Of mortals here below:
May I its great importance learn,
  It's sov'reign virtue know.

CHORUS.

Religion's more than life to me,
  It's all my soul desires;
It sets my captive spirit free,
  And lifts my soul up higher.

2 More needful this than glit'ring wealth
  Or aught the world bestows;
Not reputation, food, or health,
  Can give us such repose.

3 Religion should our thoughts engage,
  Amidst our youthful bloom;
Twill fit us for declining age,
  And for the awful tomb.

4 Let deep repentence, faith, and love,
  Be joined with godly fear;
And all my conversation prove,
  My heart to be sincere.

CHORUS.

O how I love religion,
O how I love religion,
O how I love religion,
I love it in my soul.

66   8s & 7s.

Saviour, Visit thy Plantation.

1 SAVIOUR, visit thy plantation,
    Grant us, Lord, a gracious rain,
All will come to desolation,
    Unless thou return again.

CHORUS.

Lord, revive us, Lord, revive us,
    All our help must come from thee,
Lord, revive us, Lord, revive us,
    All our help must come from thee

2 Keep no longer at a distance,
    Shine upon us from on high;
Lest for want of thy assistance,
    Every plant should droop and die.

3 Surely, once thy garden flourished,
    Every plant looked gay and green;
Then thy word our spirits nourished;
    Happy seasons we have seen.

4 But a drouth has since succeeded,
    And a sad decline we see:
Lord, thy help is greatly needed,
    Help can only come from thee.

CHORUS.

I am bound for the kingdom,
Will you go to Glory with me?
Hallelujah, praise ye the Lord.

67   8s & 7s.   ROBINSON

Rejoicing Before the Cross.

1 SWEET the moments, rich in blessing,
   Which before the cross I spend;
Life, and health, and peace possessing,
   From the sinner's dying Friend.

CHORUS.

I love Jesus, I love Jesus
   I love Jesus; yes I do;
He's my Saviour, hallelujah!
   Jesus smiles, and loves me too.

2 Truly blessed is this station,
   Low before the cross I lie;
While I see divine compassion,
   Beaming in his gracious eye.

3 Love and grief my heart dividing,
   With my tears his feet I'll bathe;
Constant still in faith abiding,
   Life deriving from his death.

4 May I still enjoy this feeling,
   Still to my Redeemer go;
Prove his wounds the source of healing,
   And himself more truly know.

CHORUS.

(To Chi dren of.)
I'll praise God, and you'll praise God
   And we'll all praise God together;
I'll praise the Lord for the work that he has
     done,
And we'll bless his name forever.

68 L. M WATTS

Pleading for Pardon.

1 SHOW pity, Lord, O Lord, forgive,
Let a repenting rebel live;
Are not thy mercies large and free?
May not a sinner trust in thee?

CHORUS.

I love the Lord, for he first loved me;
And he died on the cross for sinners.

2 O wash my soul from every sin,
And make my guilty conscience clean;
Here on my heart the burden lies,
And past offenses pain my eyes.

3 My lips with shame my sins confess,
Against thy law, against thy grace:
Lord, should thy judgment grow severe,
I am condemned, but thou art clear.

4 Yet save a trembling sinner, Lord,
Whose hope, still hovering round thy word
Would light on some sweet promise there
Some sure support against despair.

CHORUS.

(*To Show Pity, Lord.*)

O pity me, dear Saviour!
If there's any mercy, Lord,
O send it down to me,
And I'll sing halle-hallelujah!

69   P. M.   Mrs. Slade.

Footsteps of Jesus.

1 Sweetly, Lord, have we heard the calling,
    Come, follow me!
And we see where thy footprints falling
    Lead us to thee.

CHORUS.

Footprints of Jesus, that make the pathway glow;
We will follow the steps of Jesus wherever they
    go.

2 Though they lead o'er the cold dark mountains,
    Seeking his sheep;
Or along by Siloam's fountains,
    Helping the weak.

3 If they lead through the temple holy,
    Preaching the word;
Or in homes of the poor and lowly,
    Serving the Lord.

4 Though, dear Lord, in thy pathway keeping,
    We follow thee;
Through the gloom of that place of weeping,
    Gethsemane!

5 By and by, through the shining portals,
    Turning our feet,
We shall walk with the glad immortals,
    Heaven's golden streets.

D4

70   8s & 7.   RICE.

Beyond the River.

1 SHALL we meet beyond the river,
    Where the surges cease to roll?
Where, in all the bright forever,
    Sorrow shall ne'er press the soul?

CHORUS.

Shall we meet, shall we meet,
    Shall we meet beyond the river?
Shall we meet beyond the river,
    Where the surges cease to roll!

2 Shall we meet in that blest harbor,
    When our stormy voyage is o'er?
Shall we meet and cast the anchor
    By the fair celestial shore?

3 Shall we meet with Christ, our Saviour,
    When he comes to claim his own?
Shall we know his blessed favor,
    And sit down upon his throne?

CHORUS.

(*To Any C. M.*)

A Saviour, let creation sing;
A Saviour, let all heaven ring;
He's God with us, we feel him ours;
His fulness in our souls he pours;
'Tis almost done, 'tis almost o'er;
We're joining those who're gone before;
We then shall meet to part no more.

71   8s & 7s.

Shall We Gather at the River.

1 SHALL we gather at the river,
   Where bright angel feet have trod,
With its crystal tide forever
   Flowing by the throne of God?

CHORUS.

Yes, we'll gather at the river,
   The beautiful, the beautiful river,
Gather with the Saints at the river,
   That flows by the throne of God.

2 On the margin of the river,
   Washing up its silver spray,
We will walk and worship ever
   All the happy, golden day.

3 At the smiling of the river,
   Mirror of the Saviour's face,
Saints whom death shall never sever,
   Lift their songs of saving grace.

4 Soon we'll reach the shining river,
   Soon our pilgrimage will cease,
Soon our happy hearts will quiver
   With the melody of peace.

CHORUS.
(*To O When Shall.*)

O how charming; how charming!
How charming is Jesus!
He is my redeemer,
My Lord and my God.

72

C. M.

Salvation.

1 SALVATION! O the joyful sound,
'Tis pleasure to our ears;
A sovereign balm for every wound,
A cordial for our fears.

CHORUS.

I do believe; I now believe,
That Jesus died for me;
That Jesus died for all mankind,
Yes, Jesus died for me.

2 Buried in sorrow and in sin,
At hell's dark door we lay;
But we arise by grace divine,
To see a heavenly day.

3 Salvation! let the echo fly
The spacious earth around,
While all the armies of the sky
Conspire to raise the sound.

CHORUS.

Don't talk about sorrowing here below,
Let's talk about loving Jesus;
Jesus my all to heaven is gone,
And I'll sing glory, glory;
He whom I fix my hopes upon,
While marching on to glory.

73 7s. WESLEY

Sinners Turn.

1 SINNERS, turn; why will ye die?
God, your Maker, asks you why;
God, who did your being give,
Made you with himself to live.

CHORUS.

O turn, sinner, turn,
May the Lord help you turn,
O turn, sinner, turn,
Why will you die?

2 Sinners, turn; why will ye die?
God, your Saviour, asks you why?
Why, ye ransomed sinners, why
Will ye slight his grace and die?

3 Sinners, turn; why will ye die?
God the Spirit, asks you why;
O ye dying sinners, why,
Why will ye forever die?

SONG—CHORUS.

I have a Saviour (Father, etc.,) over yonder,
I have a Saviour over yonder,
I have a Saviour over yonder,
On the other bright shore.
O, bless the Lord, I want to go there,
O, bless the Lord, I want to go there,
O, bless the Lord, I want to go there,
On the other bright shore.

74   C. M.   HOSKINS.

Behold the Lamb.

1 SINNERS, behold the Lamb of God,
Who takes away our guilt:
Look to the precious, priceless blood,
That Jews and Gentiles spilt.

CHORUS.

And is there now no other way
To Canaan's peaceful ground?
Christ is the only way to God,
None other can be found.

2 From heaven he came to seek and save,
Leaving his blest abode;
To ransom us himself he gave:
"Behold the Lamb of God!"

3 He came to take the sinner's place,
And shed his precious blood:
Let Adam's guilty, ruined race
"Behold the Lamb of God!"

4 Sinners, to Jesus then draw near,
Invited by his word;
The chief of sinners need not fear:
"Behold the Lamb of God!"

5 Spirit of grace, to us apply
Immanuel's precious blood;
That we may, with thy saints on high,
"Behold the Lamb of God."

75

P. M.

In the Arms of Jesus.

1 Safe in the arms of Jesus,
  Safe on his gentle breast,
There by his love o'er shadowed,
  Sweetly my soul shall rest;
Hark! 'tis the voice of angels,
  Borne in a song to me,
Over the fields of glory,
  Over the jasper sea.

CHORUS.

Safe in the arms of Jesus,
  Safe on his gentle breast,
There by his love o'er shadowed,
  Sweetly my soul shall rest.

2 Safe in the arms of Jesus,
  Safe from corroding care,
Safe from the world's temptations,
  Sin cannot harm me there.
Free from the blight of sorrow,
  Free from my doubts and fears;
Only a few more trials,
  Only a few more tears!

3 Jesus, my heart's dear refuge,
  Jesus has died for me;
Firm on the Rock of Ages,
  Ever my trust shall be.
Here let me wait with patience,
  Wait till the night is o'er;
Wait till I see the morning
  Break on the golden shore.

S. M.   L. McWherter.

Salvation's Free.

1 SALVATION's free, indeed,
   Yes, free to one and all;
Then sinners, turn to him, and live,
   Nor spurn the Saviour's call.

CHORUS.

   I'm glad salvation's free,
   I'm glad salvation's free;
   Salvation's free, for you and me,
   I'm glad salvation's free.

2 Christ died to save the lost;
   The lost to him must fly;
There's refuge in no other name,
   It's come to him, or die.

3 But, coming, you are saved,
   All hell cannot prevent;
Salvation to a dying world,
   Is just what Jesus sent.

4 Ho! every one that thirsts,
   Salvation's waters flow,
And whosoever will, may come,
   Nor price, nor money show.

5 Repent, believe and live—
   Salvation's the new birth;
"Look unto me, and be ye saved,
   All ye ends of the earth."

77 7s.

The Comforts of Religion.

1 'Tis religion that can give,
Sweetest pleasure while we live;
'Tis religion must supply,
Solid comfort when we die.

CHORUS.

Shout, shout, we're gaining ground,
    Oh, halle-hallelujah!
The love of God is a coming down,
    Oh, glory hallelujah!
It has come down, and it will come down,
    Oh, halle-hallelujah!
It has come down, and it will come down.
    Oh, glory hallelujah!

2 After death its joys will be
Lasting as eternity!
Be the living God my friend,
Then my bliss shall never end.

SONG—CHORUS.

I have a father (mother, etc.) in the Promised
        Land,
I have a father in the Promised Land;
My father calls me, and I must go,
To meet him in the Promised Land.
I'll away, I'll away, to the Promised Land,
I'll away, I'll away, to the Promised Land;
My father calls me, and I will go
To meet him in the Promised Land.

4*

78 P. M.

The Christian Railroad.

1 THE road to heaven by Christ was made,
Of gospel truths the rails are laid ;
From earth to heaven this line extends,
To life eternal where it ends.

CHORUS.

We're traveling home—we're traveling home,
We're traveling home to heaven above.
We're traveling home to heaven above,
To sing a saviour's dying love.

2 The Bible is the Engineer,
It points the way to heaven so clear—
Through tunnels dark and dreary here,
It doth the way to glory steer.

3 The spirit's fire, as true as steel,
Which drives the engine and the wheel;
All you, who would to glory ride,
Must come to Christ, in him abide.

4 Come on, poor sinners—now's the time !
At any station on this line,
If you'll repent, and turn from sin,
This train will stop, and take you in.

CHORUS.

(*To* Come Thou Fount.)

Hallelujah ! hallelujah !
We are on our journey home;
Hallelujah ! hallelujah !
Jesus smiles, and bids us come.

79   9s & 8s.

Fatherland.

1 THERE is a place where my hopes are stayed
  My heart and my treasure are there;
Where verdure and blossoms never fade,
  And fields are eternally fair.

CHORUS.

That blissful place is my father-land,
  By faith its delights I explore;
Come, favor my flight, angelic band,
  And waft me in peace to the shore.

2 There is a place where the angels dwell,
  A pure and peaceful abode;
The joys of that place no tongue can tell—
  But there is the palace of God!

3 There is a place where my friends are gone.
  Who suffer'd and worshipp'd with me;
Exalted with Christ, high on his throne,
  The King in his beauty they see.

4 There is a place where I hope to live,
  When life and its labors are o'er;
A place which the Lord to me will give,
  And then I shall sorrow no more.

CHORUS.

(*To Jesus My All.*)

To that land, to that land, to that land I am
      bound,
Where there's no more stormy clouds arising.

80   6s, 4s & 7s.

The Happy Land.

1 THERE is a happy land,
    Far, far away,
Where saints in glory stand,
    Bright, bright as day;
O, how they sweetly sing,
Worthy is our Saviour King,
Loud let his praises ring,
    Praise, evermore.

2 Come to that happy land,
    Come, come away;
Why will ye doubting stand,
    Why still delay?
O, we shall happy be,
When, from sin and sorrow free,
Lord, we shall live with thee,
    Blest, evermore.

3 Bright, in that happy land,
    Beams every eye,
Kept by a Father's hand,
    Love cannot die.
O, then, to glory run,
Be a crown and kingdom won;
And bright above the sun,
    Reign evermore!

CHORUS.

(*To Oh, When Shall, Etc.*)

Shout, O glory! for I shall mount above the
    skies,
When I hear the trumpet sound in that morn-
    ing.

81 P. M.

Sweet By-and-By.

1 THERE's a land that is fairer than day,
  And by faith we may see it afar;
For the Father waits over the way,
  To prepare us a dwelling-place there.

CHORUS.

In the sweet by-and-by, in the sweet by-and-by,
  We shall meet on that beautiful shore.

2 We shall sing on that beautiful shore
  The melodious songs of the blest,
And our spirits shall sorrow no more
  In that home of the soul's perfect rest.

3 To our bountiful Father above,
  We will offer the tribute of praise,
For the glorious gift of his love,
  And the blessings that hallow our days.

CHORUS
(*To Jesus My All.*)

Jesus my all to heaven is gone,
  And when we get to heaven we will part no
    more;
He whom I fix my hopes upon
  And when we get to heaven we will part no
    more.
So fare you well, so fare you well,
  . And when we get to heaven we will part no
    more;
We will part no more, we will part no more,
  And when we get to heaven we will part no
    more.

82   C. M.   COWPER.

The Fountain.

1 THERE is a fountain filled with plood,
  Drawn from Immanuel's veins;
And sinners plunged beneath that flood,
  Lose all their guilty stains.

2 The dying thief rejoiced to see
  That fountain in his day;
O may I there, though vile as he,
  Wash all my sins away.

3 Thou dying Lamb, thy precious blood
  Shall never lose its power,
'Till all the ransomed Church of God
  Are saved, to sin no more.

4 E'er since, by faith, I saw the stream
  Thy flowing wounds supply,
Redeeming love has been my theme,
  And shall be 'till I die.

5 And when this feeble, faltering tongue
  Lies silent in the grave,
Then, in a nobler, sweeter song,
  I'll sing thy power to save.

CHORUS.

(*To I'm Glad that I.*)

March on, and we shall gain the victory,
March on, and we shall gain the day;
And we shall gain the victory,
And we shall gain the day.

83   C. M.   MRS. STEELE.

The Saviour Calls.

1 THE Saviour calls—let every ear
    Attend the heavenly sound:
Ye doubting souls, dismiss your fear,
    Hope smiles reviving round.

CHORUS.

Come home, come home, my child, come home,
Come to your Father's House;
    And I'll sing hallelujah,
    And you'll sing hallelujah,
    And we'll all sing hallelujah,
When we arrive at home.

2 For every thirsty, longing heart,
    Here streams of bounty flow,
And life, and health, and bliss impart,
    To banish mortal woe.

3 Ye sinners, come, 'tis mercy s voice;
    That gracious voice obey:
'Tis Jesus calls to heavenly joys,
    And can you yet delay?

4 Dear Saviour, draw reluctant hearts;
    To thee let sinners fly,
And take the bliss thy love imparts,
    And drink, and never die.

84 C. M. STOCKTON.

The Great Physician.

1 The great Physician now is near,
  The sympathizing Jesus;
He speaks the drooping heart to cheer,
  O, hear the voice of Jesus.

CHORUS.

  "Sweetest note in seraph song,
    Sweetest name on mortal tongue,
  Sweetest carol ever sung,
    Jesus, blessed Jesus."

2 Your many sins are all forgiven,
  O, hear the voice of Jesus;
Go on your way in peace to heaven,
  And wear a crown with Jesus.

3 All glory to the dying Lamb!
  I now believe in Jesus;
I love the blessed Saviour's name,
  I love the name of Jesus.

4 "The children too, both great and small,
  Who love the name of Jesus,
May now accept the gracious call,
  To work and live for Jesus."

5 And when to that bright world above,
  We rise to see our Jesus,
We'll sing around the throne of love,
  His name, the name of Jesus.

85 C. M. WATTS.

The Land of Pure Delight.

1 THERE is a land of pure delight,
　Where saints immortal reign;
Infinite day excludes the night,
　And pleasures banish pain.

CHORUS.

　I want to go, I want to go,
　　I want to go there too;
　Where social joys my heart shall fill,
　　I want to go there too.

2 There everlasting spring abides,
　And never-withering flowers;
Death, like a narrow sea, divides
　This heavenly land from ours.

3 Sweet fields beyond the swelling flood,
　Stand dressed in living green;
So to the Jews old Canaan stood,
　While Jordan rolled between.

4 Could we but climb where Moses stood,
　And view the landscape o'er,
Not Jordan's stream, nor death's cold flood
　Should fright us from the shore.

CHORUS.

O, the good old way, it's the righteous way;
I hope to die in the good old way.
　　D2

L. M.

Time Speeds Away.

1 TIME speeds away, away, away,
Another hour, another day,
Another month, another year,
Drop from us like the leafless sear;
Drop like the life-blood from our hearts
The rose-bloom from the cheek departs,
The tresses from the temples fall,
The eye grows dim and strange to all.

2 Time speeds away, away, away,
Like torrent in the stormy day,'
He undermines the stately tower,
Uproots the tree and snaps the flower,
And sweeps from our distracted breast,
The friends that loved, the friends that
        blessed,
And leaves us weeping on the shore,
To which they can return no more.

3 Time speeds away, away, away,
O, sinner turn, no more delay,
A fearful and an awful doom,
Awaits you just beyond the tomb.
The door will shut, make haste, make haste,
In outer darkness you'll be cast;
Then what will be your fearful state,
To hear pronounced, too late, too late.

The New " Over There."

1 They have reached the sunny shore,
And will never hunger more:
    All their grief and pains are o'er, over there;
And they need no lamp by night,
For their day is always bright,
    And their Saviour is their light, over there.

CHORUS. .

    Over there, over there,
    They can never know a fear, over there;
      All their streets are shining gold,
      And their glory is untold,
    'Tis the Saviour's blissful fold, over
      there.

2 Now they feel no chilling blast,
For their winter time is past,
    And their summers always last. over there;
They can never know a fear,
For the Saviour's always near,
    And with them is endless cheer, over there.

3 They have fought the weary fight,
Jesus saved them by his might,
    Now they dwell with him in light, over
        there;
Soon we'll reach the shining strand,
But we'll wait our Lord's command,
    'Till we see his beck'ning hand, over there.

88

C. M.

That Delightful Place.

1 'Twas told me in my early day,
That pleasure's stream did flow
Gently beside life's peaceful way—
I have not found it so.

CHORUS.

O that place, that delightful place,
The place where Jesus is;
The place where the Christians all shall
meet,
Shall meet, to part no more.

2 I thought there grew on earthly ground
Some buds without decay;
But not a single flower I've found
That does not fade away.

3 I wish to see a fairer world:
I've heard of one on high,
Where every tear, by one kind hand,
Is wiped from every eye.

4 'Tis said the King of that bright place
Still welcomes travelers there:
O come, and let us seek his grace!
Unseen, he hears our prayer.

CHORUS.

(*To Alas! and Did.*)

Arise, mourner, believe in the Lord,
And you won't want to stay forever here.

89 9s. JAMESON.

Heavenly Mansions.

1 There are mansions prepared in the skies,
   By the Saviour who passed on before;
And the Christian, whenever he dies,
   Finds a home where the saints die no more.

CHORUS.

Happy home, happy home, happy home, happy
      home,
Happy home, where the saints die no more;
Happy home, happy home, happy home, happy
      home,
Happy home, where the saints die no more.

2 There the Father of mercy abides,
   Whom the saints and the angels adore,
And the river of life gently glides
   From his throne in that world ever more.

3 There the Lamb that was slain, ever lives,
   In the light of the glory of God,
And to all who obey him, he gives
   Robes made white in his own precious blood.

4 There are mansions prepared for us all,
   And the Saviour is calling us home;
Sinners, harken! the Bride joins the call:
   Come to-day, for the Spirit says come!

CHORUS.

(*To Any S. M.*)

Then, sinners, freely come,
   To Jesus freely come;
He died to seek and save the lost,
   And all may freely come.

90

P. M.

To Glory I Will Go.

1 WHEN I set out for glory,
  I left the world behind,
Determined for a City,
  That's out of sight, to find.

CHORUS.

And to glory I will go,
And to glory I will go, I'll go, I'll go,
And to glory I will go.

2 I left my worldly honor,
  I left my worldly fame,
I left my young companions,
  And with them my good name.

3 Some said I'd better tarry,
  They thought I was too young,
For to prepare for dying,
  But that was all my theme.

4 The richest man I ever saw,
  Was one that begg'd the most;
His soul was filled with glory,
  And with the Holy Ghost.

5 And now we are encourag'd,
  Come, let us travel on,
Until we join the angels,
  And sing the holy song.

Revive Us Again.

1 We praise thee, O God! for the Son of thy
    love,
For Jesus who died, and is now gone above.

CHORUS.

Hallelujah! thine the glory, hallelujah! amen.
Hallelujah! thine the glory, revive us again.

2 We praise thee, O God! for thy Spirit of light,
Who has shown us our Saviour, and scattered
    our night.

3 All glory and praise to the Lamb that was slain,
Who has borne all our sins, and cleansed every
    stain.

4 All glory and praise to the God of all grace,
Who has bought us, and sought us, and guided
    our ways.

5 Revive us again; fill each heart with thy love;
May each soul be re-kindled with fire from
    above.

CHORUS.

Sing along, shout along,
Ye heaven born soldiers;
Sing along, and shout along,
And pray by the way.
Fear not, brethren,
And don't grow weary,
And never get tired
Or waiting on the Lord.

9s & 7s.

On the Ocean.

1 WE are out on the ocean sailing,
　Homeward bound, we sweetly glide.
We are out on the ocean sailing,
　To a home beyond the tide.

CHORUS.

All the storms will soon be over,
Then we'll anchor in the harbor.
We are out on the ocean sailing,
To a home beyond the tide.

2 Millions now are safely landed,
　Over on that golden shore;
Millions more are on their journey,
　Yet there's room for millions more.

3 Spread your sails, while heavenly breezes,
　Gently waft our vessel on;
All on board are sweetly singing,
　Free salvation is their song.

4 You have kindred over yonder,
　Over on that happy shore;
By and by we'll swell the number,
　When the trials of life are o'er.

5 When we're all safely landed,
　Over on that golden shore,
We will join the blood-washed millions,
　And we'll sing forever more.

93

7s.

When Shall We Meet.

1 WHEN shall we all meet again,
When shall we all meet again?
Oft shall glowing hope expire,
Oft shall wearied love retire,
Oft shall death and sorrow reign,
Ere we all shall meet again.

2 Though in distant lands we sigh,
Parched beneath the hostile sky;
Though the deep between us rolls,
Friendship shall unite our souls;
And in fancy's wide domain,
There shall we all meet again.

3 When the dreams of life are fled,
When its wasted lamps are dead;
When in cold oblivion's shade,
Beauty, wealth, and fame are laid,
Where immortal spirits reign,
There may we all meet again.

CHORUS.

O, the Lamb, the loving Lamb,
The Lamb of Calvary;
The Lamb that was slain,
And liveth again,
To intercede for me.
And O, give him glory,
For glory is his own.

94   P. M.

The Old Ship of Zion.

1 WHAT ship is this that will take us all home,
    O glory, hallelujah.
What ship is this that will take us all home,
    O glory, hallelujah.
  'Tis the old ship of Zion, hallelujah,
  'Tis the old ship of Zion, hallelujah.

2 Do you think she will be able to take us all
    home, etc.,
Do you think she will be able to take us all
    home, etc.?
  I know she will be able, hallelujah,
  I know she will be able, hallelujah.

3 Come along, come along, and let us go
    home, etc.,
Come along, come along, and let us go home, etc.
  Our home is over Jordan, hallelujah,
  Our home is over Jordan, hallelujah,

4 What kind of freight have you on board, etc.,
What kind of freight have you on board, etc.
  Love to God, and one another, hallelujah,
  Love to God, and one another, hallelujah.

5 We have some friends before us gone, etc
We have some friends before us gone, etc
  By and by we'll go and meet them, hallelujah,
  By and by we'll go and meet them, hallelujah.

.6 And we'll walk up and down the golden
    shore, etc.,
And we'll walk up and down the golden shore,
    etc.,
  And we'll praise the Lord, forever, hallelujah,
  And we'll praise the Lord, forever, hallelujah.

P. M.

A Call to Work.

1 Work, for the night is coming,
  Work through the morning hours;
Work while the dew is sparkling,
  Word 'mid springing flowers;
Work when the day grows brighter,
  Work in the glowing sun;
Work, for the night is coming,
  When man's work is done.

2 Work, for the night is coming,
  Work through the sunny noon;
Fill brightest hours with labor,
  Rest comes sure and soon;
Give every flying moment,
  Something to keep in store;
Work, for the night is coming,
  When man works no more.

SONG—CHORUS.

I have a father (mother, etc.) in the Promised
    Land,
I have a father in the Promised Land;
I hope one day we'll all get there,
Away over in the Promised Land.
Away over in the Promised Land,
Away over in the Promised Land;
I hope one day we'll all get there,
Away over in the Promised Land.
They must be mighty happy in the Promised Land
They must be mighty happy in the Promised
    Land;
And I hope one day we'll all get there,
Away over in the Promised Land.

96

Wondrous Love.

1 WHAT wondrous love is this,
    O my soul!
That caused the Lord of bliss
To bear the dreadful curse
    For my soul?

2 When I was sinking down,
    Sinking down,
Beneath God's righteous frown,
Christ laid aside his crown,
    For my soul.

3 Ye winged seraphs, fly,
    Bear the news;
Like comets through the sky,
Fill vast eternity
    With the news.

4 Ye friends of Zion's King,
    Join his praise;
With hearts and voices sing,
And strike each tuneful string
    In his·praise.

5 To God and to the Lamb
    I will sing;
Who is the great I AM,
While millions join the theme,
    I will sing.

97 L. M. STENNETT.

Meeting With Christ.

1 WHERE two or three, with sweet accord,
Obedient to their sovereign Lord,
Meet to recount his acts of grace,
And offer solemn prayer and praise.

CHORUS.

O glory, hallelujah!
Praise him, hallelujah!
Glory, hallelujah,
Praise ye the Lord!

2 There will the gracious Saviour be,
To bless the little company;
There, to unvail his smiling face,
And bid his glories fill the place.

3 We meet at thy command, O Lord!
Relying on thy faithful word;
Now send the Spirit from above,
And fill our hearts with heavenly love.

CHORUS.

(To Jesus My All.)

My Father's in heaven—I want to go there,
  Halle-hallelujah!
My Father's in heaven—I want to go there,
  O glory, hallelujah!
Why don't you go on? you're pretty near there,
  Halle-hallelujah!
Why don't you go on? you're pretty near there,
  O glory, hallelujah!

98 6s.

Give me Jesus.

1 WHILE wandering to and fro,
In this wide world of woe,
Where streams of sorrow flow—

CHORUS

Give me Jesus—give me Jesus
Give me Jesus;
You may have all this world—
But give me Jesus;

2 When tears o'erflow mine eye,
When pressed by grief I sigh,
Still this shall be my cry—

3 When to the mercy seat
I go, my Lord to meet,
My heart shall still repeat—

4 And when my faith is tried,
In him will I confide,
And all the storms outride—

5 Though strength and friends should fail,
And foes my soul assail,
Through him I shall prevail—

6 And when my toils are o'er,
When nearing Jordan's shore,
I'll shout, as up I soar—

C. M. WATTS.

Inspiring Hope.

1 WHEN I can read my title clear,
   To mansions in the skies,
I'll bid farewell to every fear,
   And wipe my weeping eyes.

CHORUS.

I want to go, I want to go,
I want to go there too;
Where social joy my heart shall fill,
I want to go there too.

2 Should earth against my soul engage,
   And fiery darts be hurled,
Then I can smile at Satan's rage,
   And face a frowning world.

3 Let cares, like a wild deluge, come,
   Let storms of sorrow fall;
So I but safely reach my home,
   My God, my heaven, my all.

4 There I shall bathe my weary soul
   In seas of heavenly rest,
And not a wave of trouble roll
   Across my peaceful breast,

CHORUS.

(*To When I Can Read.*)

We are passing away,
We are passing away,
We are passing away
To that great Judgment Day.

100 C. M. Steele

The Royal Feast.

1 YE wretched, hungry, starving poor,
  Behold a royal feast!
Where mercy spreads her bounteous store,
  For every humble guest.

CHORUS.

  Then sinner, come, to Jesus come;
    Come to this royal feast:
  Come eat, and live, no longer roam,
    Come, be a regal guest.

2 See, Jesus stands with open arms;
  He calls, he bids you come:
O stay not back, though fear alarms!
  For yet there still is room.

3 O come, and with his children taste
  The blessings of his love;
While hope attends the sweet repast
  Of nobler joys above!

4 There, with united heart and voice,
  Before th' eternal throne,
Ten thousand thousand souls rejoice,
  In ecstacies unknown.

5 And yet ten thousand thousand more,
  Are welcome still to come:
Ye happy souls, the grace adore;
  Approach, there yet is room.

ALPHABETICAL INDEX.

(Reference to number of Hymn.)

ALPHABETICAL INDEX.

ALPHABETICAL INDEX.

ALPHABETICAL INDEX.

TO SONG—CHORUSES.

CPSIA information can be obtained
at www.ICGtesting.com
Printed in the USA
BVHW081529210119
538277BV00020B/927/P

THE
TOTNES TO ASHBURTON RAILWAY
(and The Totnes Quay Line)

by

Anthony R. Kingdom

ARK PUBLICATIONS (RAILWAYS)

First published in 1995 by ARK PUBLICATIONS (RAILWAYS), an imprint of
FOREST PUBLISHING, Woodstock, Liverton, Newton Abbot, Devon TQ12 6JJ

British Library Cataloguing in Publication Data
A catalogue record for this book is available from the British Library
ISBN 1–873029–02–0

0–4–2T No. 1427 taking on water at Totnes whilst on duty on the Ashburton Branch
R. S. Carpenter

ARK PUBLICATIONS (RAILWAYS)
Editorial and design by:
Mike Lang

Typeset by:
Carnaby Typesetting, Torquay, Devon TQ1 1EG

Printed and bound in Great Britain by:
BPC Wheatons Ltd, Exeter, Devon EX2 8RP

Cover photographs:

Front — (Top)   0–4–2T No. 1470 pulls back into Totnes Station, after taking water
from the column between the up platform line and the up main line,
and prior to uncoupling, running around the single coach (an
ordinary brake composite) and preparing for the return journey to
Ashburton on 25th October, 1958.   *Peter W. Gray*

(Lower)   0–4–2T No. 1427 pulls away from Ashburton Station with the
single coach train to Totnes on 25th October, 1958, just one week
before the regular British Railways passenger service on the branch
was terminated.   *Peter W. Gray*

Back –   The tranquil scene on the outskirts of Buckfastleigh as the 'down'
train from Totnes, headed by 0–4–2T No. 1427, crosses the River
Dart to begin the final stage of its journey to Ashburton on 11th
October, 1958.

Peter W. Gray

CONTENTS

ACKNOWLEDGEMENTS

The author wishes to extend his grateful thanks to the following for their generous assistance, given in a wide variety of ways during the preparation of this book:

British Rail, Western Region; Dart Valley Light Railway Co.; Dart Valley Railway Association; Dartington Hall Trust; Devon County Records Office, Exeter; Great Western Society Ltd; Mid-Devon Advertiser, Newton Abbot; Nicholas Horne Ltd, Totnes; Plymouth City Library; Plymouth Railway Circle; Signalling Records Society; South Devon Railway Trust; Totnes Borough Museum; Totnes Times & Guardian; Western Independent; Western Evening Herald; Western Morning News.

J. Allen; J. Anning; J. B. N. Ashford; H. Aylott; J. B. Cogar; L. R. Dinwiddy; C. Fennamore; B. Gibson; P. W. Gray; J. Heggadon; P. J. Isaac; C. Judge; B. Kohring; P. A. Lemar; L. Littleton; H. Pitts; P. J. Powell; C. Richardson; R. C. Sambourne; R. Taylor; S. Taylor; F. Thatcher; K. Williams; W. A. Wright.

Special thanks are due to the Dart Valley Railway Co. for permission to carry out surveys and research on their property, and also to Mr. L. R. Dinwiddy, the former station-master at Buckfastleigh, for the information on traffic and staffing contained in the chapter 'Time Tables and Branch Working'

(Photographs are acknowledged individually except those taken by the author or from his own collection)

FOREWORD

Having been associated with the Ashburton Branch since 1920 when I became a member of the staff at Buckfastleigh and as the last Station Master there when the Branch was finally closed in 1962, I was delighted when asked to write a foreword to the short history of the Branch.

In my younger days it seemed the local railway station became one of the focal points of country life. It is a matter of regret that the internal (or infernal) combustion engine gradually weaned traffic away from the Railways until it became fairly obvious the future of Branch lines as feeders to the main line were coming to an end.

There was a short period of reanimation during the war years when Railways became the handmaiden of wartime transport requirements, but with the return of peace, the decline in rail traffic continued and no-one was greatly surprised when the axe finally fell.

All who have used the Branch agree it would be hard to find a more beautiful stretch of scenery than is found on the 7 miles between Buckfastleigh and Totnes, when the train literally meanders along the banks of the River Dart for practically the whole distance.

This is really emphasised by the fact the Dart Valley Railway was formed to purchase the line and operate it as a tourist attraction with, of course, Great Western Steam Locomotives. Thousands of tourists now take a trip to enjoy the scenery from along the banks of one of England's most beautiful rivers.

Mr. Kingdom's short history will be of great interest to many past and present users of the line.

1st March 1976   R.R. Dinwiddy J.P.

Mr. L. R. Dinwiddy, for many years stationmaster of Buckfastleigh and the last stationmaster on the branch.

Devonshire Press, Torquay

4

PREFACE

When the fore-runner to this book, *The Ashburton Branch,* was conceived by the Oxford Publishing Company and written by me during 1975/6 the 'Railway Preservation Lobby' was in full swing, and the Dart Valley Railway was well established between Totnes and Buckfastleigh. Both the Publisher and I thought that this was a bonus for publishing the book and that it would effectively stimulate its sale.

We were hopelessly wrong, however, for quite the reverse proved to the the case! Sales of the book were inhibited by the presence on the market of a plethora of publications 'about the Dart Valley': prospective customers thought that this was "just another ". *The Ashburton Branch* then had the dubious distinction of being the slowest selling of the popular series of branchline histories produced by the O.P.C. at that time.

Now, some 18 years later, the pendulum has swung completely, and second-hand copies, when they are available, are sold for up to eight times their original 1977 cover price of £2.40.

It was this fact, coupled with the increasing demand for the history of this popular line, that prompted the proprietors of Forest Publishing and I to update and republish this work.

This new edition is largely a reprint of the original book except for additional information and photographs that I have been able to include since it first appeared. A few minor errors have also been corrected, and a superb map of the branch inserted to supplement the complete OS mapping of the line.

We feel confident that this updated and revised reprint of *The Ashburton Branch,* under its new title *The Totnes to Ashburton Railway,* will delight those who failed to obtain a copy the first time around. In doing so we hope to have given pleasure to those interested in a part of Devon's extensive transport history.

Anthony R. Kingdom
Thalassa
Newton Ferrers
Devon
January 1995

INTRODUCTION

The Ashburton Branch's history was firmly cemented into the early history of the railways of Devon and its life was both chequered and varied, even though its closure was comparatively early in terms of the Beeching era. Nevertheless, closure was still late enough for memories to dwell lucidly in the minds of those who worked and travelled on the line, and the task of research was helped considerably by this fact. At the same time, however, I do not wish to imply that the maintenance of accuracy was made any easier because of this: I have endeavoured to make the text as accurate as possible,

5

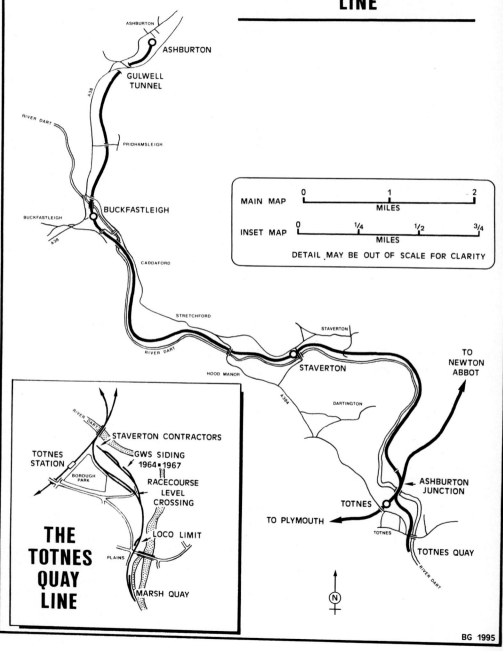

THE
TOTNES AND ASHBURTON
LINE

ASHBURTON

ASHBURTON

GULWELL TUNNEL

A 38

RIVER DART

PRIDHAMSLEIGH

BUCKFASTLEIGH

BUCKFASTLEIGH

A 38

CADDAFORD

STRETCHFORD

RIVER DART

STAVERTON

STAVERTON

HOOD MANOR

A 384

DARTINGTON

TO NEWTON ABBOT

MAIN MAP	0	1	2
		MILES	

INSET MAP	0	1/4	1/2	3/4
		MILES		

DETAIL MAY BE OUT OF SCALE FOR CLARITY

TOTNES

TO PLYMOUTH

ASHBURTON JUNCTION

TOTNES

TOTNES QUAY

RIVER DART

THE TOTNES QUAY LINE

RIVER DART

TOTNES STATION

BOROUGH PARK

STAVERTON CONTRACTORS

GWS SIDING 1964 ■ 1967

RACECOURSE LEVEL CROSSING

LOCO LIMIT

PLAINS

MARSH QUAY

N

BG 1995

but alas, no-one is infallible and for any errors that may occur, I do apologise in advance.

The branch started life in 1872 as the Buckfastleigh, Totnes & South Devon Railway, and was a 9½ mile spur in broad gauge branching off the South Devon Railway main line from Exeter to Plymouth, just east of Totnes. It existed thus, worked by the South Devon Railway, for 25 years until absorbed by the Great Western Railway in 1897, during which time it had been converted to the standard 4' 8½" gauge.

The Totnes Quay Line, however, was much more obscure to research possibly due to its lowly status in life. It began as a horse drawn goods line and continued so until 1874. Even when locomotives were permitted upon it, they were allowed only as far as the level crossing onto The Plains. The section past the level crossing, known as 'Tram Gate', continued to be horse drawn until 1948, whereupon it was taken in the charge of a tractor for the rest of its working life.

The G.W.R. ran the branches successfully until nationalisation, when they changed to public ownership and became part of British Railways. The constant competition of the motor car in the post-war years forced the Ashburton branch to close to passengers after more than 75 years of service. Further decline in goods traffic caused its complete closure in 1962.

It was at this time that a group of businessmen were negotiating the purchase of the branch to run as a private railway and tourist attraction. It was at this time also, the Great Western Society had formed the nucleus of a live steam museum on the sidings adjacent to the Quay Line. This was achieved by the kind permission of the then Totnes Borough Council and Staverton Contractors Ltd.

It was envisaged that this newly formed Society would represent enthusiast support of the light railway company, but due to many technicalities, this sadly did not come about. Instead the Dart Valley Railway Association was formed to support the company and the Great Western Society moved to Didcot on the subsequent closure of the Quay Line. Its stock, which had been moved in part to Buckfastleigh in anticipation, was then withdrawn except for No 1369, which was handed over to the Dart Valley Railway.

The Dart Valley Light Railway was finally established and took over the running of the Totnes to Buckfastleigh section exclusively in 1969. It had also leased the section to Ashburton but, despite many further and prolonged negotiations to consolidate it, failed to save it from destruction.

This section has now become the foundation of part of the new A38, four lane carriageway running from Plymouth to Exeter, by-passing both Ashburton and Buckfastleigh en route.

One must be thankful, however, that the most beautiful part of the line from Totnes to Buckfastleigh survived its centenary. In these days of the 'concrete jungle', one hopes that, here at least, Great Western steam will continue to flourish beside the lovely River Dart for another hundred years!

Anthony R. Kingdom

Aerial view of Totnes looking roughly east, showing 'A', the start of the Ashburton branch and site of the D.V.L.R. 'Totnes Riverside' station; 'B' shows the start of the Quay line and 'C' the main line to Newton Abbot.

Nicholas Horne Ltd.

THE ROUTE DESCRIBED

Totnes to Ashburton. The route described.

Much to my regret, I cannot claim to have travelled the Ashburton branch either in the halcyon days of the Great Western or the post nationalisation days of British Railways. I shall attempt however, to describe a trip along its nine miles and twenty chains as one might have experienced such a journey in the late 'fifties, just before its closure.

The junction for Ashburton was of course, Totnes, an elongated main line station whose track layout stretched roughly over half a mile, from M.P.223¼ in the west to M.P.222¾ in the east.

Totnes station is situated in the north west corner of the town, dominated in its earlier years by the square tower of the old atmospheric pumping station for the abortive attempt at silent traction by the then South Devon Railway. In later years, this dominance was to succumb to the round erect factory chimney of Daw's (later still, Unigate's) Creameries.

Through the station ran four sets of tracks, the 'up' and 'down' through roads for all excursion and non stopping trains, including the through goods trains. Either side of these were the 'up' and 'down' platform lines running closer to their respective platforms and catering for all stopping trains. It was to and from these platforms, the Ashburton branch trains arrived and departed.

Half way along the 'up' platform stands the signal box with its one hundred and eleven lever frame working to Tigley in the west and Dainton in the east. The signal box did not always stand here, it was in fact, built in 1932 to replace a similar one occupying a corresponding position on the opposite platform. The replacement signal box was not the only change in the history of the station, its faces were indeed many during its hundred years of existence.

The original station, built for the South Devon Railway was of a lateral timber planking construction with an overall roof spanning both the 'up' and the 'down' Platform lines.

The two platforms were connected by a covered footbridge of an iron lattice type, covered with a corrugated iron roof. During the passage of time, the roofs of both station and footbridge have disappeared in subsequent re-buildings.

9

Scene at the height of the fire on the down side of Totnes station during the early hours of Saturday, 14th April 1962.

Nicholas Horne Ltd., C'ty J. Falmer

View of Totnes station exterior on its 'down' side, showing the replacement buildings used as 'Ticket Office/Waiting Room' and a 'Refreshment Room' following the fire of April 1962. Photograph 19th January 1967.

10   British Rail (W.R.)

Its present construction is a mixture of both old and new and nothing has been done to remove the austerity of this main line station. It is still basically timber built in wide lateral planking, formerly employed in its original construction. The old overall roofs, which were supported in the 'six foot' by large square pillars of timber, one foot or more thick, have been replaced. The more usual canopies of corrugated iron panels, supported by iron brackets, trimmed with a vertical facia of wood cut in a 'saw tooth' pattern, are now in evidence.

(The entrance on the southern side was later extensively rebuilt in a most unattractive manner, following a serious fire which occurred in the early hours of Saturday, April 14th, 1962. The fire destroyed the Booking Office and Hall, the Parcels Office and Refreshment Room. These were quickly replaced with temporary prefabricated buildings, brought from Plymouth the following day, and are those still in situ today! Despite this, it had that homely, welcoming atmosphere, typical of so many Westcountry stations of the Victorian era.)

To offset the austerity of the station, passengers had nearby, the grounds of Borough Park with the well kept flower beds and swings for the children. This lovely little park is situated directly opposite the southern entrance of the station, whilst the two together are overlooked away to the south west by the ruins of Totnes Castle.

To the eastern end of the 'down' platform, stands a goods shed, also of timber construction and containing two roads, one equipped with a loading gauge and crane, the latter mounted inside on the loading dock. (During 1965 this goods shed was demolished.)

Various track layouts existed during the long life of Totnes station, as was common with most of its contemporaries. The main eras could be loosely divided into a) the late 1890s, b) the early 1930s and c) the late 1960s. However, two factors remained constant at the eastern end of the station through most of its history and consequent track re-arrangements. These were the departure from the 'up' main line, of the Ashburton Branch in a northerly direction just short of M.P. 222½ and the departure from the 'down' main line of the Totnes Quay Line in a southerly direction just short of M.P.222¾.

With the aforegoing assessment of Totnes station concluded, the journey to Ashburton can now be contemplated. An 0-4-2 Tank and two autocoaches stand patiently waiting for the 'off' on the 'up' platform line after shunting operations had been completed, following the alighting of passengers on the 'down' platform from an earlier trip.

On being given the road by the 'up platform starter', the train pulls out of the platform to pick up the main line, though for a very short period. This will allow the crossing by bridge of the river Dart, flowing on a south westerly course just east of the station boundary.

Immediately having crossed the bridge and passing the branch starting signal, Ashburton Junction is encountered and the main line is quickly forsaken for the branch proper. It is interesting to note that originally a signal box stood in the angle the branch made with the main line, until 1933. At that time it was closed and control of the branch was transferred to Totnes signal box, where it has remained ever since.

Leaving the main line, the branch takes a meandering course in a roughly northerly direction, crossing many small embankments which allow passengers a good view of the weir to the west. During this time M.P.½ is passed and the line runs under the small stone Hampstead bridge carrying a farm track from Hampstead farm to its more southerly fields. Running over the slightly rising ground, the course of the river Dart is quickly emulated as the branch 'up home' is passed midway to M.P.¾. A further series of small embankments punctuate the next stretch of line running in a north easterly direction past M.P.'s 1 & 1¼. Between these mileposts stand the Totnes 'up distant' signal and again, it is interesting to note that here stood more than one 'Royal Train' on a visit to the Westcountry. Quite secluded from the main line and heavily guarded, royal personages could live and sleep safely between engagements around the county.

A clear view of the river and Aller Park School is seen to the west as the train proceeds. The river's erratic course contrasts strongly with this very straight stretch of line as it approaches Parsonage Wood and platelayers hut 1. Here the embankment gives way to higher ground on its eastern flank as it skirts the length of the wood passing M.P.1½.

Leaving the northern end of Parsonage Wood, the line changes to a more westerly course as it passes beneath Parsonage Manor house to the east, with Winton House standing in its lea. The line is now literally running beside the beautiful river Dart as it enters a long banked cutting south of Staverton Wood, passing as it does M.P.1¾ and the platelayers hut 2. As M.P.2 is reached, the line swings away almost due west, still keeping adjacent to the confines of Staverton Wood to the north and the river Dart to the south. To the rear of the latter can be seen the contrasting Thistlepark Plantation of deciduous firs, namely the Larch and Spruce. Leaving the woods and passing M.P.2¼ as it does, the line runs alongside platelayers hut 3 and along a further series of embankments, passing Park Copse to the south on the last lap towards Staverton Bridge.

By the time M.P.2½ is encountered, St Paul's Church tower and clock in Staverton village can be seen to the north, whilst to the south the Town Mills are also visible from the train. The mills are situated between the river, which is rather more distant, and the line itself. Further to the south at this point, lie Staverton Ford Plantation and Chasegrove Wood.

A small road to the mills crosses the track at Mill Crossing, (sometimes known as Knapper's Crossing after the family who worked it for many years) so causing the train to slow whilst the gates were manned

A general view of Staverton in the early 1950s, looking towards Totnes.

O.P.C.

The 3.25 p.m. Totnes to Ashburton train arriving at Staverton on 19th October 1957.

R. F. Roberts

by the occupants of the crossing keepers cottage nearby. Passing under the track by this level crossing, is a culvert carrying water from the river to work the mills.

Once the train has negotiated the crossing, Staverton 'down fixed distant' and M.P.2¾ are passed as the line proceeds eastwards towards Staverton village, passing once more over the water supply to the mills by means of another culvert. At M.P.3 the line swings in a south westerly direction on a small embankment south of the large Staverton Joinery Works.

As the final approach to Staverton station is made, Staverton 'up starter' and 'down home', M.P.3¼ and platelayers hut 4 are passed in that order. The principal level crossing is situated here in the valley adjacent to the station. It provides for the crossing of the line by a minor road arriving in from the A834, Totnes to Ashburton road, at Huxham's Cross. This road passes through Staverton Bridge towards Staverton village by turning to the right and to Landscore, by turning to the left. The waters of the river Dart rush under the ancient bridge leading to the level crossing as it edges still further from the course of the line.

Staverton station lies in a valley dominated by the steeply wooded slopes of North Wood on its southern side. It has a genuine character of gentle charm consistent with an old world wayside halt. It has a single platform on the northern side of the line, behind which are situated the station buildings and goods sheds.

Adjacent to the level crossing at the eastern end of the station stands a small signal box which would be more accurately described as a covered ground frame! It is built of wooden planking vertically placed, with no less than seven window frames giving it an all round vision of the line. The apex roof is of asbestos slate finished with ridge tiles and one wall sports a full length cast iron signal box nameplate. Outside the box stands Staverton 'up home' signal.

The small station building is brick built with an apex roof of timber planking covered with slates. Four small windows overlook the platform, these being for the waiting rooms, booking office and toilets etc. The road side of the building has a central doorway with steps leading up to it and flanked by two other small windows. The doorway opens out onto a covered porch serving as a waiting area and forming the centre section of the whole building. A solitary chimney exists on the western end of the building where the battery supplies to the block telegraph are also housed in large wooden cupboards.

The two goods sheds are built in a similar manner to the station building, i.e. brick walls and slate roofs. The first goods shed is immediately to the east of the station building and in line with it. It has no windows, but has two heavy sliding doors opening out onto the platform on its southern and eastern sides. The second goods shed is situated still further to the eastern end and is set back from the building line of the station to allow for the provision of a siding, serving it on its southern side. Two heavy wooden sliding doors open out onto the loading bay, one at each end. The road side is provided with further access for loading purposes and again, access is also provided onto the platform by means of two additional sliding doors of the same type, one for the former and one for the latter. The track layout was simple, consisting of the running line, one siding leading across the level crossing serving the second goods shed, as previously mentioned, with a back up siding in the reverse direction.

Leaving Staverton Bridge on the next part of the journey to Buckfastleigh, the line continues to run south west past the old mill leat. This presents the track with another culvert to cross as it passes the 'down starter' signal, west of the station. Running south of Netherton House, M.P.3½ is reached as the line swings west again and runs almost parallel with the river.

More beautiful scenery is forthcoming as a cutting is entered south of Abraham's Wood. Proceeding on past M.P.3¾ and Staverton 'up fixed distant' the line emerges onto an embankment at M.P.4, a point which gives a panoramic view of the weir and Hood Island in the centre of the river. Indeed, this is one of the loveliest stretches of the upper Dart and is a local paradise for fishermen. To the south, Hood Manor and Hood Barton are visible just before the line passes under Riverford (also known as Hood) bridge. It is here the A384, Totnes to Ashburton road crosses the line at right angles by means of this old stone bridge, built more for transport of the horse drawn era rather than that of the motor car.

Having passed under Riverford Bridge and the accompanying platelayer's hut No 5 in the lea of its western side, the line veers north west and approaches a small cutting below Riverford House and M.P.4¼. More embankments follow in succession as M.P.'s 4½, 4¾ and platelayers hut 6 are encountered in order. The line is running side by side with the river in the flatter ground of the valley bottom, crossing over a small bridge spanning a drainage stream as it does so. It is dominated at this point by the high ground around Stretchford to the north and Hood Ball to the south.

Between M.P.5 & M.P.5¼, a longer cutting is encountered as the line swings northward following the river faithfully on its northern bank, whilst further on between M.P.5¼ & M.P.5½, platelayers hut No 7 is reached on the more steeply rising gradient.

Now commences a long straight stretch of track running almost due north, still within the flat bottomed river valley, passing between M.P.'s 5½ & 6. Just past M.P.5¾ however is situated platelayers hut No 8 on the branch. High above the line over this section are steep wooded hills, rising in some places to over 600 feet above sea level, away to the south west near Rattery and the main line.

A view of Buckfastleigh station, goods and signal box buildings during the early 1950s.

No. 1470, with a train for Totnes, waits at Buckfastleigh on 1st March 1956.

R. M. Casserley.

After M.P.6 the line returns to a more north westerly course as it negotiates a more or less continuous embankment towards the approaches to Buckfastleigh. Here Colston Road runs parallel to the line at Rill Wood to the west, whilst the A384, Totnes to Ashburton road condescends to take up company with the line again to the east. At M.P.6¼ the line passes over yet another bridge spanning a drainage stream and proceeds over the now level ground past yet another platelayers hut, No 9 in the series. Between here and M.P.6½, the line crosses the river Dart for the second time on its journey, at a point just short of Austin Bridge. Immediately after M.P.6½ stands the uncharacteristic tall concrete post of Buckfastleigh 'down distant' signal. A steep embankment follows, running closely by Kilbury Manor and Dartmill Cottages, as the line enters a deep cutting and passes under a road bridge high above carrying the old Totnes road over it. M.P.6¾ and the rear of Buckfastleigh 'up starter' appears as the line makes its way over the river Mardle, a small tributary of the Dart, and on into the outer confines of Buckfastleigh station. At this point the density of signalling increases, the 'down home', the rear of the 'up starter' and the rear of the 'loop to main' signals are passed in quick succession to both the left and right of the line. Finally as the station master's house is passed on the left, the train arrives alongside the platform at Buckfastleigh station itself.

It is a typical Great Western branch line station, situated close to the main A38, Plymouth to Exeter trunk road and lying in the valley of the river Dart. It is approximately a quarter of a mile away from Buckfastleigh to the south west and three quarters of a mile from Buckfast to the north west. "Buckfastleigh for Buckfast Abbey" the station nameboard reads, for it was in 1907 that the first stone was laid to commemorate the rebuilding of the abbey by the Catholic monks. This imposing building was not completed until as late as 1932 so, together with Truro Cathedral, it must surely qualify to being one of the youngest ecclesiastical buildings in the Westcountry. The station building is constructed of limestone edged with yellow brick and the walls give way to no less than 10 windows and 5 doors. Each of the windows are constructed of wooden frames shaped at their tops with obtuse angled apexes and mounted over slate sills. The doors, also of wood are shaped in a similar manner and number two on the platform side and three on the road or front side. The roof is of slate and forms an apex parallel with the platform and is punctuated along its length by three sturdy limestone chimney stacks, two on either end of the original building and the third on the road side of what must have been a later extension to it on the northern end.

The roof on the southern end is slightly lower than the main roof which itself gives way to the platform canopy. The canopy too follows Great Western fashion in its construction, for it is supported by seven heavy ornamental cast iron brackets, each carrying a timber beam. On top of each beam is the main fabric of the canopy, edged in the familiar way with a plain facia trimmed with a wooden skirt of short longitudinal planks, their ends cut to form a 'saw tooth' pattern.

At the southern end also stands a good example of a G.W.R. 'Pagoda', constructed wholly of corrugated iron sheeting secured to a light metal frame. It has three sets of double wooden doors and was probably used as oil/general store. The platforms are of mixed construction but mainly of limestone facing, edged with large stone slabs, the infill being earth and hardcore topped with chippings. The second platform on the 'up' side was of later construction and was not of the usual standard, its main use being the unloading of horses etc for the Buckfast races. However, the two were connected by means of a wooden 'barrow crossing' laid in the trackbed at their southern end.

The goods shed was built to match the station building, i.e. of limestone roofed with slate. It was situated in a 'set back' location at the northern end of the station, its apex roof ending with wooden planking over the track entrance, the other half limestone. The western, or road side was equipped with the usual heavy wooden doors on runners, allowing cart and lorry access to the large timber loading bay. By the side of these doors stood a brick built outbuilding housing the offices, but these were probably a later addition.

Further towards the northern end of the station confines stands the signal box directly opposite M.P.7. Its construction is of a standard brick base with wooden window frames and an asbestos slate roof covering its twenty seven lever frame.

The main platform is equipped with gas lighting, with the cast iron lamp standards holding the round Victorian enamelled lamps sporting their hanging chains and dimpled glass globes. Under the canopy the same types hang sedately on the ends of their gas supply pipes. Both platforms carried the usual seats of wooden beams supported by three cast iron frames carrying the G.W.R. monogram. The layout of track in the station included at this time three reverse sidings into loading docks, a passing loop and two facing sidings running towards the Dart river bridge, at the northern end.

Having entered Buckfastleigh in a north westerly direction, the line departs in a similar direction, curving away and crossing the river Dart for the third and last time by means of the Dart rail bridge. Just prior to crossing this bridge, the backing signal 'loop to main' and the 'down starter' are passed, one standing either side of the track. The bridge is followed by two further signals, the 'down home' bracket and the 'up advanced starter' as the line quickly passes under a road bridge carrying the A384 from Buckfast to Totnes followed by M.P.7¼.

Here the little river Ashburn passes under the embankment on its way to join the Dart east of Dart Bridge. Running almost parallel to the

A38, the line continues north west past Furzeleigh Mill, the river Ashburn flowing on its western side. From this point on towards Ashburton the line skirts the foot of a high ridge of land on its eastern flank, rising in some places in excess of 500 ft above sea level. The river Ashburn stubbornly keeps company with the line's western flank as M.P.7½, together with platelayers hut 10, are passed.

Pridhamsleigh Quarry is reached as the line proceeds over further sections of the flat bottomed valley. Away in the distance to the west, the top of the tower of the famous St Mary's (Buckfast) Abbey comes momentarily into view before being quickly obscured again by hills. As the line swings in a large curve, firstly to the north east and back again to the north west, Buckfastleigh 'up distant', M.P.7¾ are passed in order. Most of this length of line runs over a series of modest embankments, climbing steeply, excepting for a stretch between Pridhamsleigh Quarry and Pridhamsleigh Barton where the trackbed cuts into the hill on its eastern flank. North eastwards again the line passes under a bridge carrying a minor road from its junction with the A38 at Furzeleigh, over the Mill leat, the river Ashburn and the railway, to Pridhamsleigh.

Platelayers hut 11 appears next as the line runs over another modest but long embankment approaching M.P.8, on its last lap climbing steeply towards Ashburton station. Meandering around in a large curve towards the north east again, the line moves ever closer to the river Ashburn (also known as the R. Yeo) as it crosses a drainage sluice between M.P.8¼ & M.P.8½. At the latter, the site of platelayers hut 12 is reached and it will be noted that the same flat bottomed valley of the river Ashburn, is but a continuation of that of the Dart the train has followed since Buckfastleigh station. The river Dart parted company with the line there in order to find its source high upon the slopes of Dartmoor, well behind the town of Ashburton.

The last of this pleasant journey takes the train past Rosery Mount, Priestaford Farm, and the Gages, with its large orchard, on the western side of the line whilst on the eastern side is the high land capped by Woodend and Gluewell Hamlets. Before the train finally enters the confines of Ashburton station, the A38 makes a defiant swing towards the east and crosses the line at M.P.9, 'branching' as it does so into the old Totnes road and Cabbage Hill, before passing Ashburton on its eastern flank as an original by-pass. The railway line however, still faithfully keeping company with the river, runs on into the outposts of Ashburton station. Swinging almost due north, Ashburton 'down home' signal is passed following by M.P.9¼. (It is interesting to note here that Ashburton had no fixed distant signal). The old malthouse and the engine shed are then encountered on either side of the line, the sidings at the incoming end, the water tower, station outbuildings including the last of the ubiquitous platelayers huts, No 13, and lastly a ground frame.

(a)

20

(b)

(c)

(d)

Four views of Ashburton during the early 1950s showing:- (a) The exterior, complete with ancient gas street lamp and Tuckers Seed Merchants warehouses. (b) The water tower, engine shed and departing auto train. (c) The rear of the engine shed and the lines into the terminus which can be seen in the background. (d) The outside of the station buildings and forecourt. (Note the canopy, shown in earlier view, no longer exists over the forecourt.)　　　　　　　O.P.C.

No 1470 leaves Ashburton with the daily goods on a summer's day in 1956.

R.C. Riley

No 1427 pulls out of the platform line in order to pick up the second auto coach, just in view under the station roof, on 2nd July 1957.

R. C. Riley

All now give way to the platforms of Ashburton station—journey's end!

Ashburton station is situated almost in the centre of the town, bounded on the eastern side by the gas works in Parish Road and the Railway Hotel on the western side. The station building is constructed of limestone walls with an apex roof of slate similar to that of Buckfastleigh. Two limestone chimney stacks are situated at each end of the building whose frontage faces the Railway Hotel at the end of Lawrence Road. The main building consists of the usual offices for a branch line terminus, i.e. Booking Office; Station Master's Office; Waiting Room and Toilets.

Backing out onto the platform side of the building is the overall wooden roof covering both the 'up' and 'down' platforms. It consists of lateral wooden planking supported by upright timbers set in the platform on the 'up' side. (It was, in fact one of the only examples of its type still existing at the time, other than Exeter St Thomas.)

The western wall of this overall roof is formed by the rear wall of the station building. It provides seven supports for the rafters of the roof which, together with the five timber supports previously mentioned, held the roof in place. In earlier years these timber supports were vertically planked down to platform level, making the interior very dark. At the time of our journey however, the planking had for many years been reduced to one third of the way down.

The roof fabric is of timber also, diagonally planked and the whole construction is strengthened by a network of iron struts and tie bars. Louvres close to the apex are in evidence to allow for the dispersal of smoke and steam from the engines. The 'down' platform is of limestone but the 'up' platform is of brick, both are edged with large stone slabs with rounded edges. The infill is of earth and hardcore topped with tar and chippings, for the most part. Under the roofed section the platforms are paved with paving stones.

At the far end of the station, hidden from passengers, stands a corrugated iron hut used for storage of paraffin and lamps, and a small brick built store. At the southern end of the 'down' platform stands the 'platform starter' signal worked by a single lever ground frame on the platform. Behind this platform runs the siding into the goods shed, which stands just south of the station building and immediately behind the platform end, so that its limestone walls abut it and its two square windows overlook it. A round brick lined arch spans the sidings and wooden doors close over the square section of the doorway into the shed. A loading gauge stands at the rear end of the platform.

All is surveyed by two of the four benign faces of the clock of St Andrews Church in the background. Here in the quite calm of the little market town the passengers alight from the train and walk out through the exit into the fresh moorland air.

Aerial view of Totnes looking roughly south, showing the main line station and Quay line. 'A' marks the end of the Quay line; 'B' the former G.W.S. museum site and 'C' marks 'Tram Gate' level crossing over the A385 road.

Nicholas Horne Ltd

Totnes Quay Line—The route described in retrospect.

This branch left the 'down' main line just short of M.P.222¾ in a southerly direction. It quickly changed to south easterly as it crossed a metal bridge over Mill Leat and entered a deepening cutting to the east of Borough Park.

Running roughly in the same direction, the line doubled for the next part of its journey between the industrial estate built on the old Totnes Racecourse to the north east and the Pollards housing estate to the south west. The exit road from the industrial estate is then encountered by a level crossing, without gates, over both tracks.

The line took up a southerly course again and became single at the rear of Harris bacon factory. Just prior to this however, a reverse siding ran back from a point near the level crossing, to serve the industrial estate itself. This siding formerly served the Staverton engineering works, the foundry and in later years, South Devon Farmers and the Totnes Borough Council cattle market.

The last item was in turn served by another spur off the branch siding from a point just north of the level crossing and was probably altered thus at the time of the construction of the Livestock Market. (These sidings were, in final years, the home of the G.W.S. steam museum.)

Returning to the stretch of line at the rear of the bacon factory, (which had its own siding until 1964) the track singled and passed over the Mill Leat yet again. It was from this point where locomotives were not allowed to proceed further. The line then swung around to the south west as it crossed the Mill Leat for the fourth and final time, before it crossed the main A385, Totnes to Paignton road. This was another level crossing without gates, and was known as 'Tram Gate' crossing.

On the last part of its journey, the line swung in a large radial curve from its south westerly course, firstly to a southerly and then south easterly one. Here the line traversed the Plains passing on its eastern flank the warehouses that back onto Mill Tail. (A 30 ton weighbridge exists at a point half way along this warehouse complex.)

The last part of the ¾ mile long branch ran along New Walk, bordered by the large timber stores of Reeves & Co and terminates, without buffer stops, on the river Dart's western bank adjacent to St Peters Quay Pool. From these last few hundred yards, another reverse spur siding is evident. It is that of March Quay siding, complete with its own crane, running adjacent to Mill Tail where the sand barges unloaded their cargoes.

A fairly level branch, the Quay line is obviously not noted for its scenery but it would be unfair not to mention the view of the river at its point of termination. Where Mill Leat runs into the river Dart at St Peters Quay Pool, the two waterways have run either side of an elongated peninsula, known as 'The Island'. This is a delightful open

The view from the point of termination of the Quay line during the 1890s. The Mill Tail to the left, the River Dart to the right of the Island, both flowing into St. Peters Quay Pool in the foreground. Note the paddle steamer's passengers with their umbrellas!

Chapman & Son

The 1904 vintage steam paddle steamer 'Kingswear Castle' awaits further passengers during the summer of 1910.

Chapman and Son

space of tree and shrub covered land used by local inhabitants as a park and mecca for fishing enthusiasts.

Looking up river past the slipways on the opposite bank, a good view of Bridge Pool and the ancient Totnes Bridge are seen, the latter carrying the A385 over the river. Looking well down river past the wharfs and berths of the timber trade, the more rural and sylvan setting is encountered of the lower reaches of the river Dart. It is from here, the head of navigation, that the pleasure steamers leave for their journey past Dittisham and Stoke Gabriel on their way to Dartmouth and Kingswear. In days gone by, paddle steamers of the River Dart Steamboat Co plied the river with their happy cargoes of holiday makers. Their names, like the engines of the G.W.R., were those of 'Castles'. The first of these, 'Berry Castle' was an iron paddler built at Kingswear in 1880. Others were to follow bearing names such as Dartmouth Castle, Totnes Castle, Compton Castle and Cardiff Castle. In latter years these boats were replaced with others with similar names but the sad difference was they were diesel driven! Although the Totnes Quay line had no connection with the steamer traffic, the G.W.R. often issued 'round trip' tickets which offered to include a steamer trip one way on the Dart in addition to the rail journey excursion.

Steamer Quay, Totnes.

46/14

The final years of steam on the river Dart. The *'Compton and Kingswear Castles'* preparing for a trip down the river during the 1950s era. (These boats were built in 1914 and 1924 respectively.)

Overland Views, Launceston

27

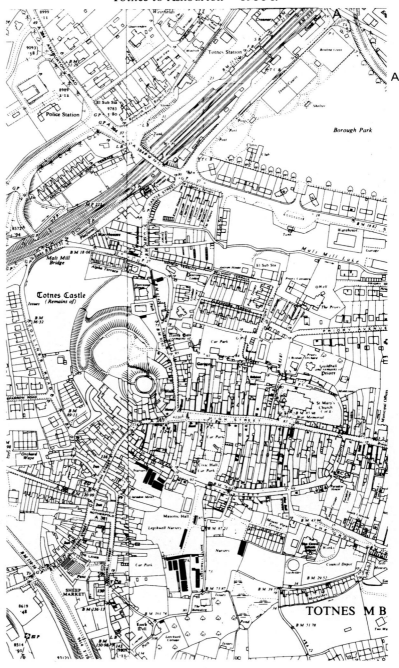

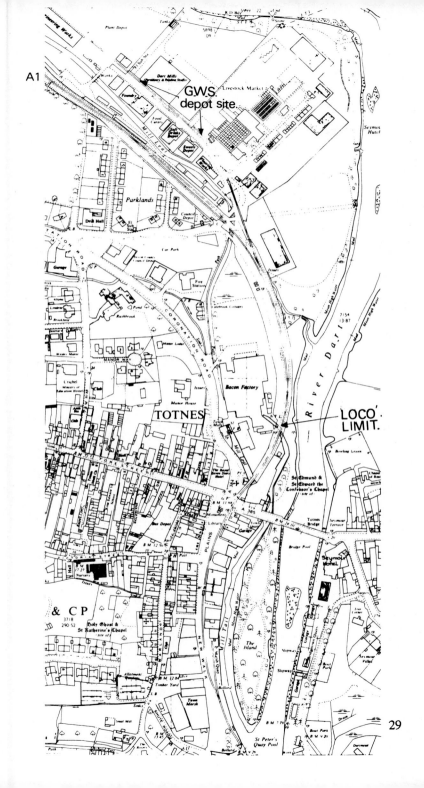

A1

G.W.S.
depot site.

Livestock Market

Parklands

TOTNES

Bacon Factory

LOCO'
LIMIT.

River Dart

& C P

29

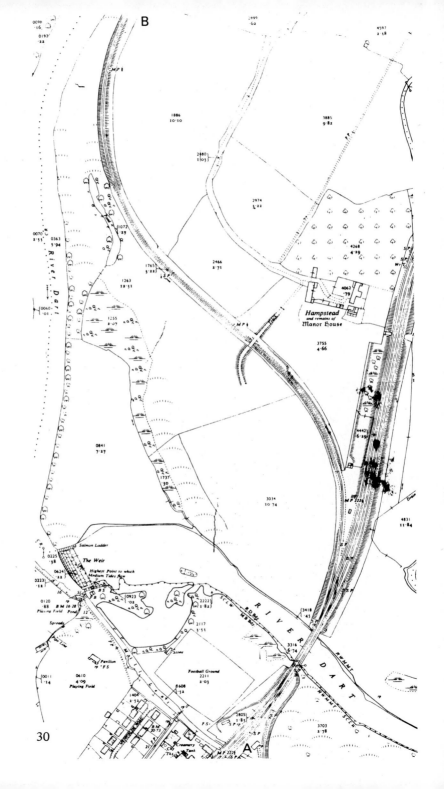

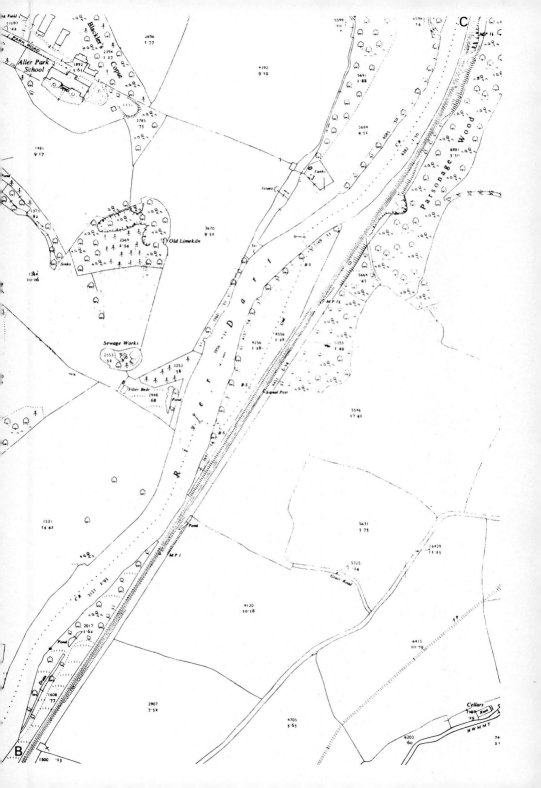

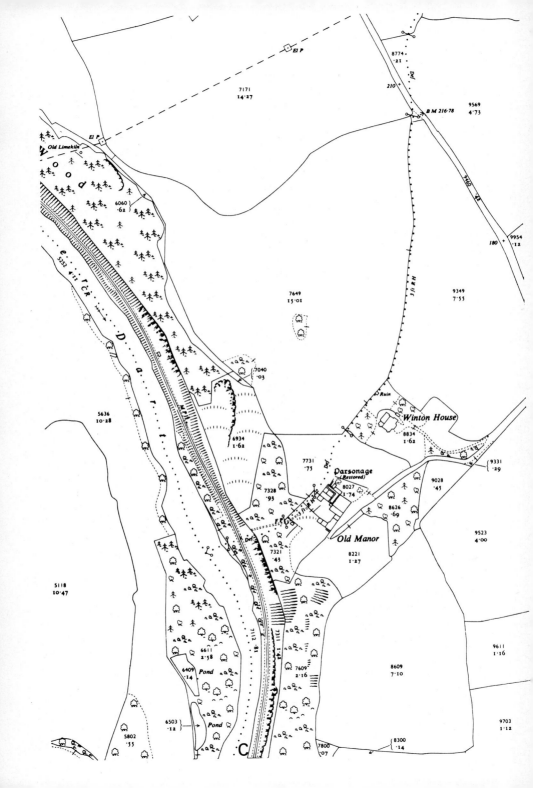

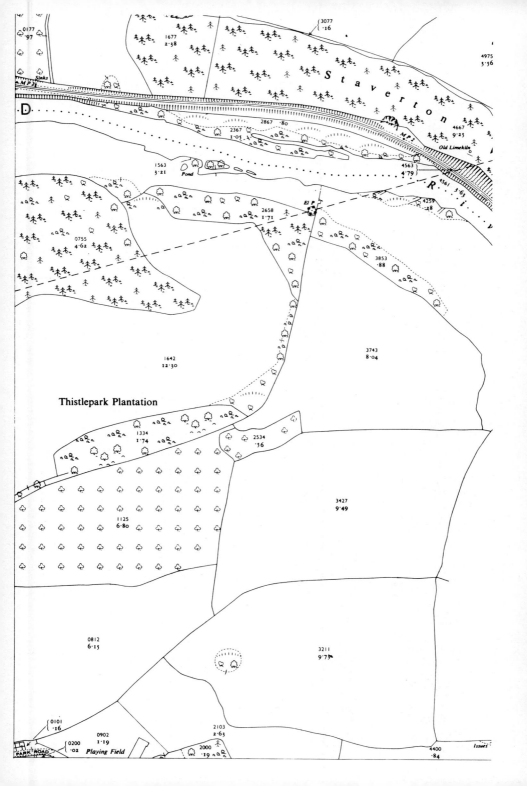

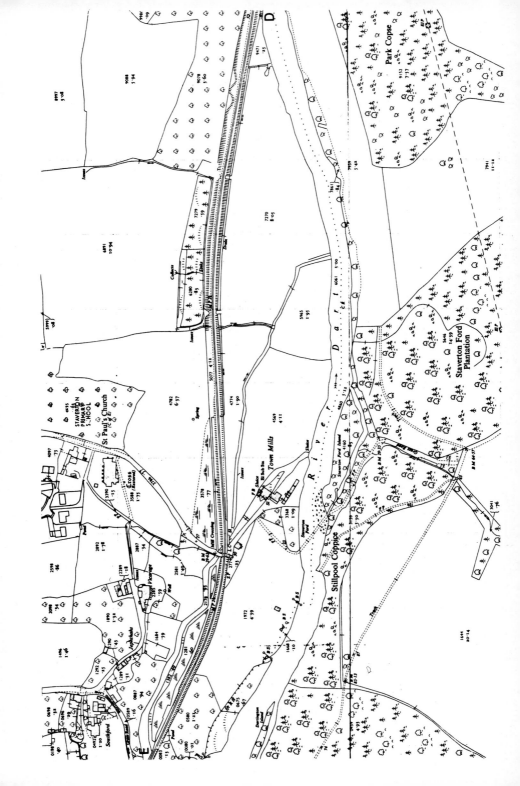

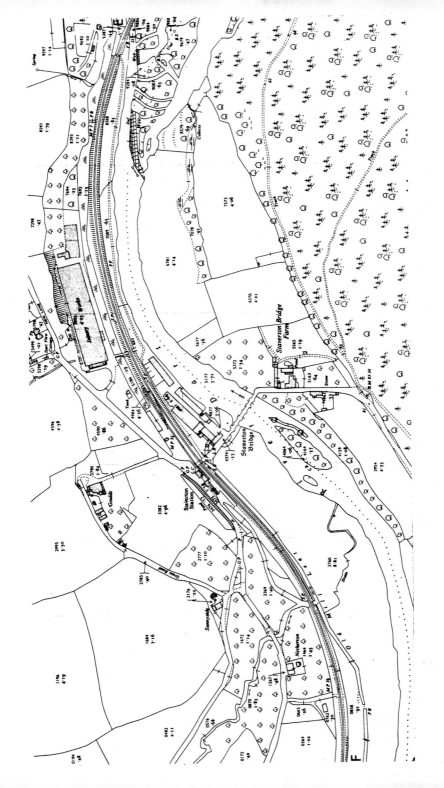

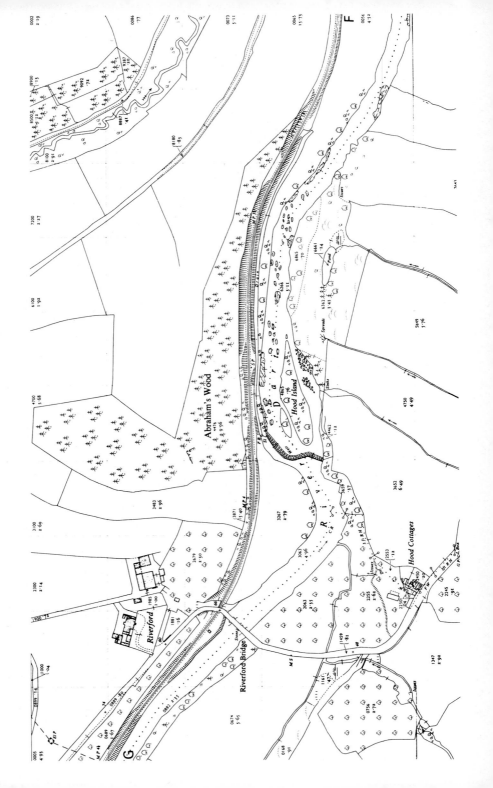

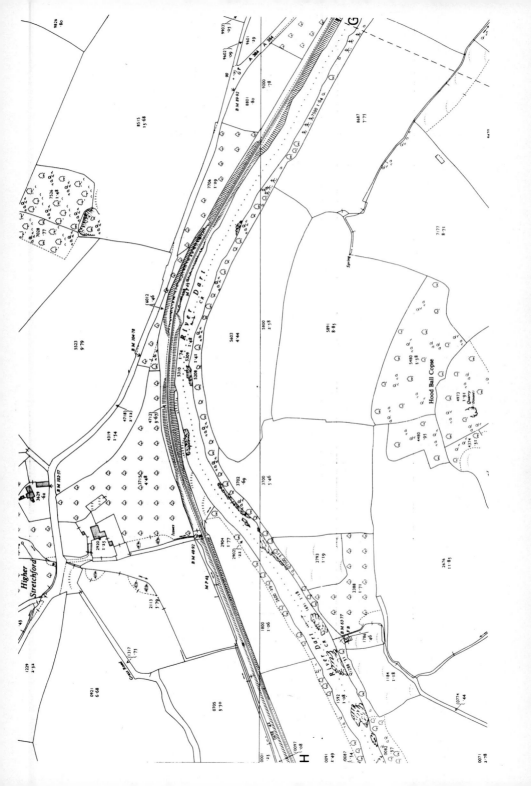

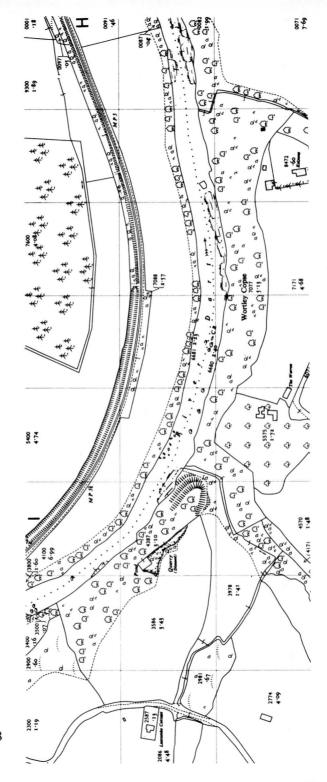

38

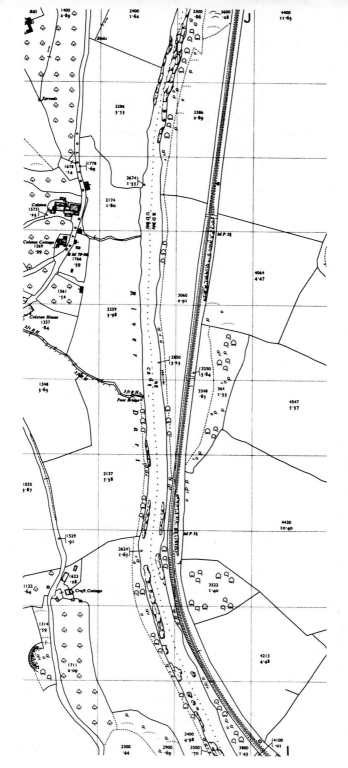

39

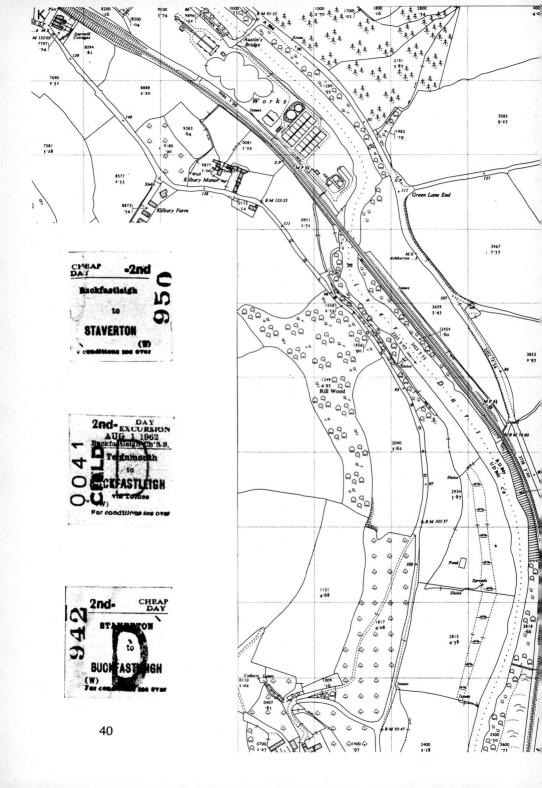

CHEAP
DAY   -2nd
Buckfastleigh
to
STAVERTON
(W)
conditions see over

950

2nd-   DAY
EXCURSION
AUG 1 1962
Buckfastleigh Ch S.S.
Teignmouth
to
BUCKFASTLEIGH
via Totnes
(W)
For conditions see over

0041 COLD

2nd-   CHEAP
DAY
STAVERTON
to
BUCKFASTLEIGH
(W)
For conditions see over

942

40

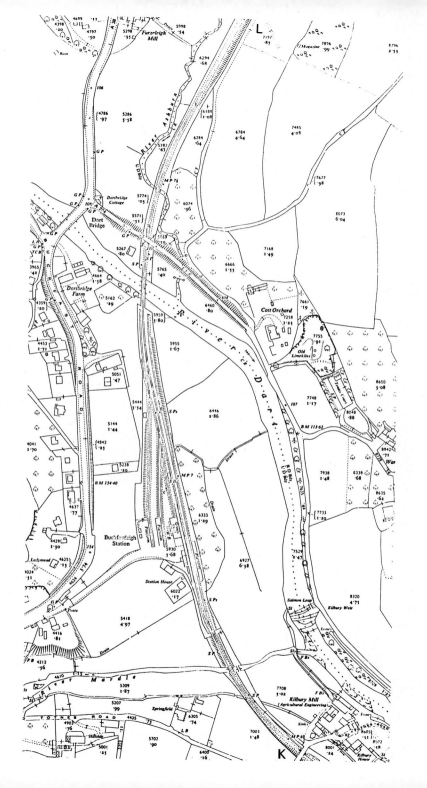

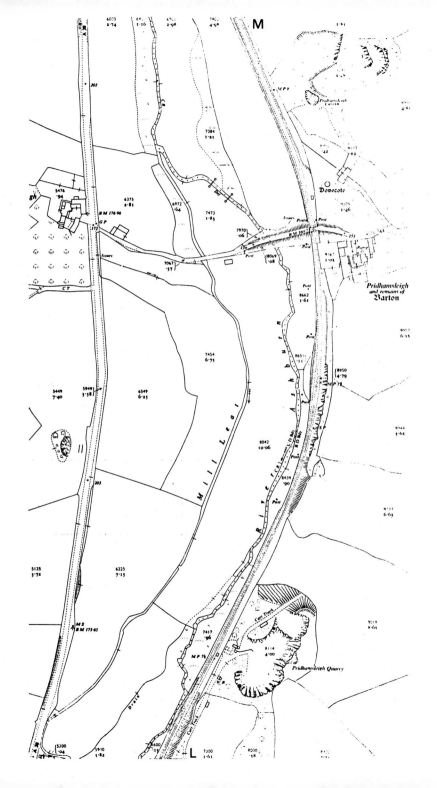

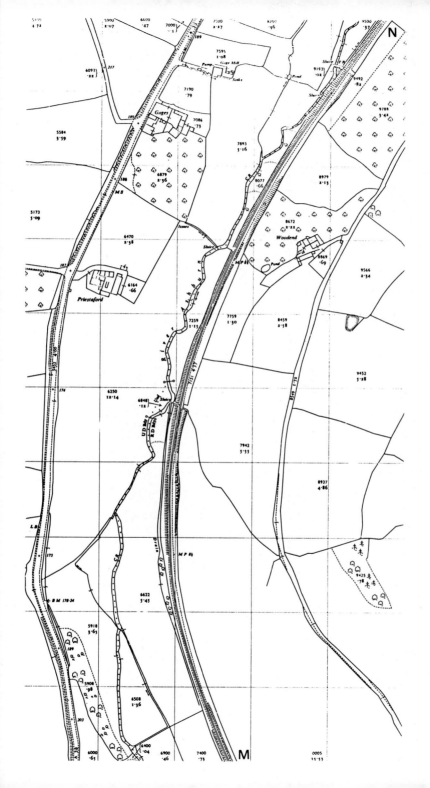

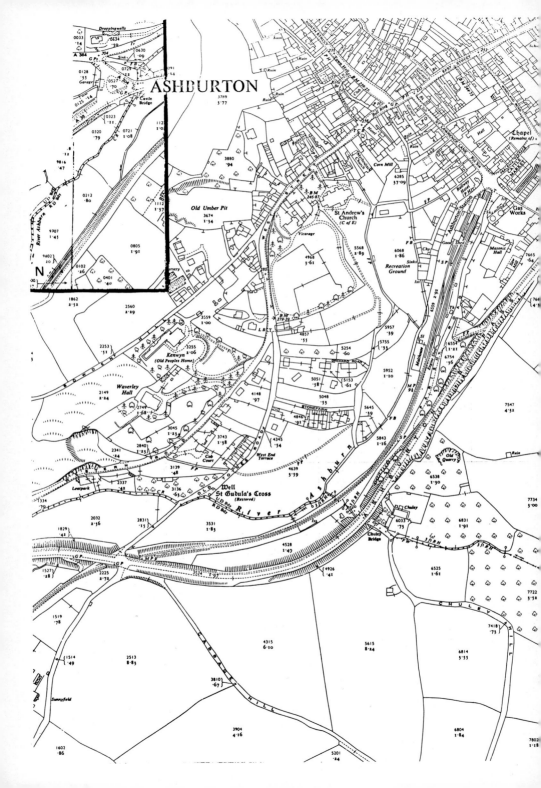

Buckfastleigh to Ashburton — 1975.

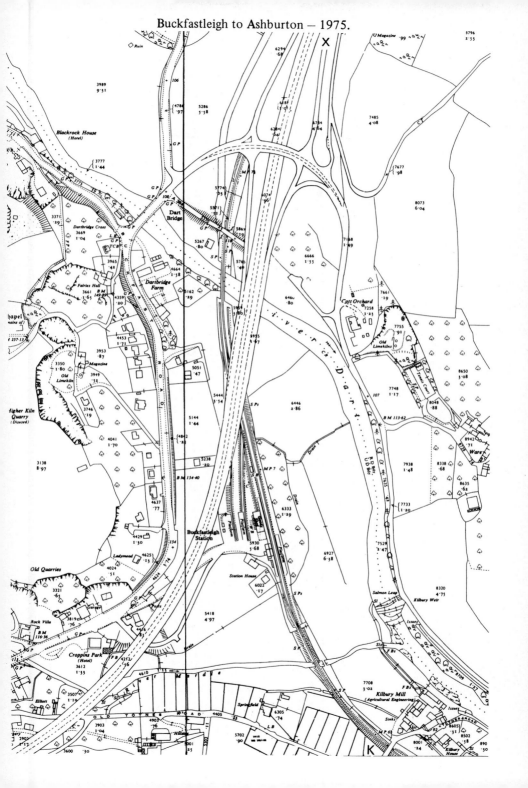

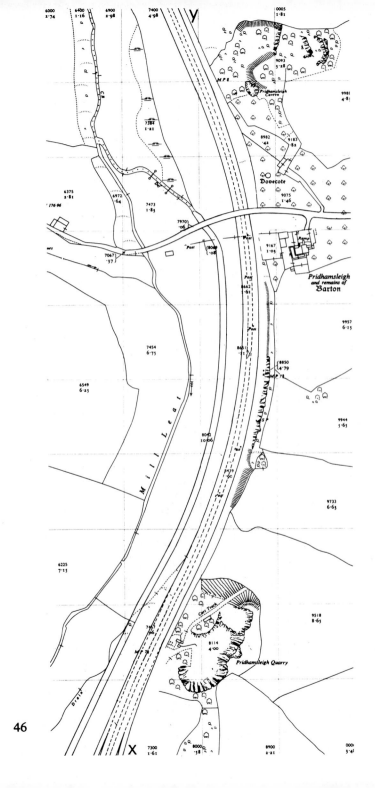

46

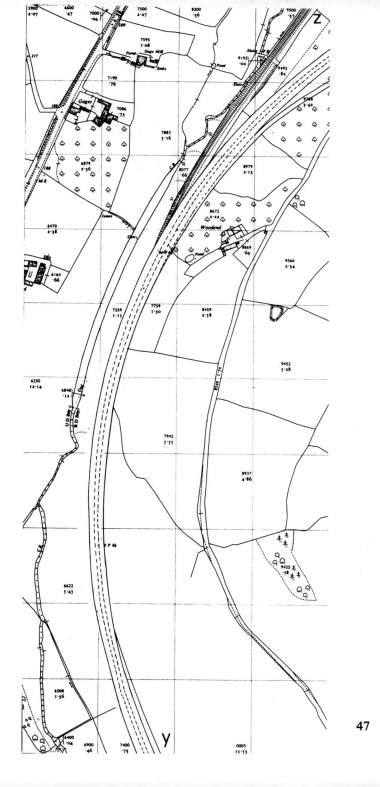

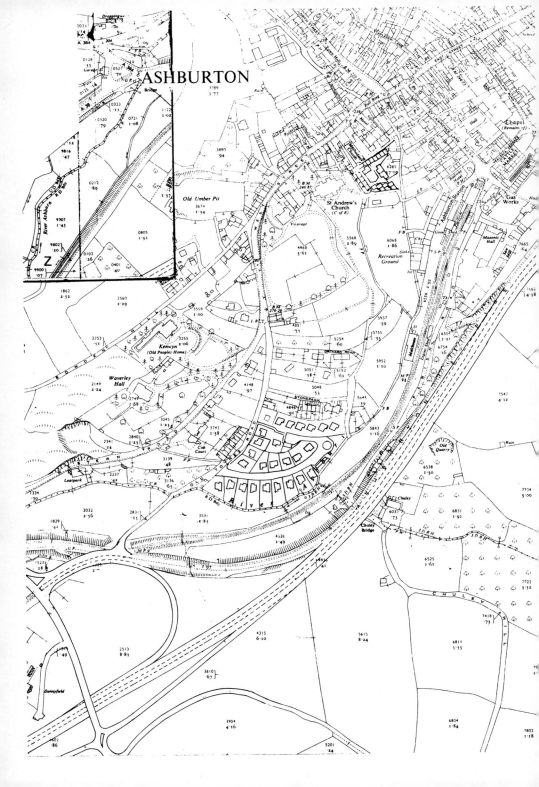

ASHBURTON

SHARE No. 622...

THE BUCKFASTLEIGH, TOTNES & SOUTH-DEVON RAILWAY COMPANY.

Incorporated, 1864.

£ 10 SHARE.

This is to Certify that Baldwin John Pollexfen Bastard

of Kitley, Yealmpton near Plymouth, Esquire

is the Proprietor of Sixteen Shares Nos. from 10 to 12 in

THE BUCKFASTLEIGH, TOTNES & SOUTH-DEVON RAILWAY COMPANY, Subject

to the Regulations and Orders of the Company.

Given under the Common Seal of the

said COMPANY the 31 day of May 1872

R J Hamlyn
John Furneaux } DIRECTORS

Alex Wedge, Secretary

BUCKFASTLEIGH, TOTNES, AND SOUTH DEVON RAILWAY

Incorporation of Company for making a Railway from the South Devon Railway at Totnes to Buckfastleigh, with a Branch to Totnes Quays—Working and traffic arrangements with South Devon Railway Company—Power to use portion of South Devon Railway and Station at Totnes—Amendment of Acts.

NOTICE IS HEREBY GIVEN that application is intended to be made to Parliament in the next session thereof for an Act to incorporate a Company, with power to make and maintain the following railways, or one of them, with all proper stations, wharves, approaches, works, and conveniences connected therewith—that is to say:

1st. A railway commencing in the parish or township of Littlehempstone, in the County of Devon, by junction with the South Devon Railway, near to the bridge which carries that railway across the River Dart, and near to the Totnes Station of the said South Devon Railway, and running thence from, through, or into the following parishes, townships, extra-parochial and other places, or some of them, viz.:— Littlehempstone, Dartington, Berry Pomeroy, Bridgetown, and Totnes, all in the County of Devon, and terminating in the Parish of Totnes, at, upon, or near the Quay belonging, or reputed to belong, to the Trustees of the Totnes Charities and in the occupation of Richard Coleridge, and at a point, 125 yards, or thereabouts, southwards of a certain store or warehouse belonging to the Trustees of the Totnes Charities aforesaid, and in the occupation of John Michelmore.

2nd. A Railway commencing in the said Parish of Littlehempstone by a junction with the South Devon Railway near to the bridge which carries that Railway across the River Dart, and near the Totnes Station of the said South Devon Railway, and running, thence from, through, or into the following parishes, townships, extra-parochial and other places, or some of them, viz.:—Littlehempstone, Totnes, Berry Pomeroy, Dartington, Staverton, Rattery, Ashburton, and Buckfastleigh, all in the County of Devon, and terminating in the Parish of Buckfastleigh, in a Field numbered 1,479 on the Tithe Map of the said Parish of Buckfastleigh, which said Field belongs, or is reputed to belong, to Thomas Michelmore, and is in the occupation of John Ball, at a point distant about 100 yards, or thereabouts, in a south-easterly direction from a bridge called Dart Bridge, which carries the turnpike road leading from Ashburton to Buckfastleigh over the River Dart.

And it is proposed by the said intended Act to empower the intended Company to purchase lands, houses, and other property by compulsion or agreement, either for a sum or sums in gross, or in consideration of annual or other payments, and to vary or extinguish all existing rights or privileges in any manner connected with such lands, houses, and property, or which would in any manner impede or interfere with the construction, maintenance, or use of the said intended Railways and works, and to confer other rights and privileges: and also to take powers to cross, stop up, or divert, whether temporarily or permanently, all such turnpike and other roads, railways, tramways, aquaducts, cuts, canals, streams, navigations, and rivers within or adjoining to the aforesaid parishes, townships, and extra-parochial or other places, or any of them, as may be necessary in consequence of the construction, and for the purposes of the said intended Railways and works.

And it is further proposed by the intended Act to authorise the levying of tolls, rates, and charges for the use of the said intended Railways and works, and to confer exemptions from the payment of such tolls, rates, and charges, and to confer all other usual and necessary powers.

50

And it is also proposed by the intended Act to empower the Company, and the South Devon Railway Company to enter into agreements or arrangements for the working, maintenance, and use by the last-named Company of the intended Railways and works, or any part thereof respectively, and the supply and maintenance of engines, carriages, and rolling stock, and other stock or plant for the same; and with respect to the payment and contribution by the Companies towards the costs, charges, and expenses of such working use, management, and maintenance; and with respect to the conduct, regulation, management and transmission of the traffic upon the intended Railways, and the Railways of the South Devon Railway Company, and the stations, works, and conveniences connected therewith respectively and with respect to the levying; collection, payment, division, apportionment, appropriation, and distribution of the tolls, rates and charges arising from such respective traffic, and the tolls, charges, or other considerations to be paid for such use or otherwise and to enable the South Devon Railway Company to levy tolls, rates and charges on the said intended Railways, or any part thereof; and to exercise all such other powers as may be found advisable in reference to the purposes aforesaid; and the intended Act will provide, if thought fit, for the appointment of a Joint Committee, and for the confirmation of any agreement entered into in relation to all or any of the matters aforesaid.

And it is also proposed by the intended Act to empower the Company thereby to be incorporated, and all other Companies and persons lawfully using their Railways, or either of them to pass over and use with their engines and carriages of every description, and with their clerks, officers, and servants, upon such terms and conditions, and on payment of such tolls, rates, and charges, or other consideration, as may be agreed upon or settled by arbitration, or provided for in the intended Act, so much of the South Devon Railway as is situate between the junctions therewith of the intended Railways respectively and the Station and the watering places, water, booking-offices, sidings, works, and conveniences connected therewith respectively.

And it is also proposed by the intended Act, so far as may be necessary for the purposes aforesaid, to alter, amend, and enlarge, the powers and provisions of the Act 7 and 8 Vic, cap. 68 and any other Act or Acts relating to the South Devon Railway Company.

Duplicate plans and sections shewing the lines and levels of the proposed Railways and other works with a book of reference to such plans, containing the names of the owners, lessees, and occupiers of the lands intended to be taken; a published map, with the lines of Railway delineated therein, so as to shew their general course and direction; and a copy of this notice as published in the *London Gazette*, will on or before the 30th day of November instant, be deposited for public inspection with the Clerk of the Peace for the said County of Devon, at his Office in the Castle of Exeter; and on or before the same day a copy of so much of the plans, sections, and book reference, as related to each parish, and a copy of this notice will be deposited with the Parish Clerk of each such parish, at his residence; and in the case of any extra-parochial place, with the Parish-Clerk of an adjoining parish, at his place of abode.

Printed copies of the proposed Bill will be deposited in the Private Bill-Office of the House of Commons on or before the 23rd day of December next.

Dated this 13th day of November, 1863.

H. MICHELMORE, Newton Abbot;

SWIFT & CO., 32, Great George-street, Westminster.

1045   Solicitors for the said Bill.

THE ASHBURTON & TOTNES QUAY BRANCHES—
HISTORY

Phase I. — 1845 to 1872/3. Conception to their opening.

It is a popular conception that most branch lines which met their fate
by closure, were once profitable concerns and only the advent of the
motor car or nationalisation were responsible for their demise. This
theory is not wholly true, for some were never profitable concerns and
often great sacrifices were made by the inhabitants of the rural areas
wherein they ran, to facilitate their construction in the first place.
Sadly, it has to be admitted, the Totnes to Ashburton branch fell into
this category.

Initially an act of November 1845 provided for the original main line
of the Plymouth, Devonport & Exeter Railway to be routed via
Buckfastleigh and Ashburton and plans were deposited with the Devon
authorities setting out the proposed route. This line was to leave
Plymouth via Plympton, St Mary/St Maurice, passing the rear of
Lyneham Lodge and Smithaleigh, passing through the following parishes
en route to Exeter.—(It was to be constructed in the reverse direction.)
South of Ivybridge—Ermington—Ugborough—South of Aish (S. Brent)—
Dean Prior—south of Dart Bridge (B'leigh parish)—Ashburton, (23 miles
from Plymouth)—Staverton (North of Pridhamsleigh)—Bickington—
Islington—south of Teigngrace—Kingsteignton—thence along the borders
of the parishes of Hannock/Chudleigh—Christow/Trusham/Ashton—
Bridford/Doddiscombe Holcombe—Burnel—Dunsford—Ide—Alphington
—St Thomas (Exeter), finally crossing the South Devon Railway near
the river Exe and into the site of which was to become Exeter, Queen
St (later Central) of the L.S.W.R. Here a connection was to join onto
the S.D.R. proper. History has shown however this route was not to be
for various reasons, outside the scope of this book.

A scheme was also projected during 1845 to link Ashburton to
Newton (Abbot*) directly by rail and it was to be known as the
Ashburton, Newton & South Devon Jucn Railway, having its connection
with the main line as its name suggested, at Newton (Abbot*).

Miscellaneous records of meetings regarding this railway include the
following extracts:
"At a numerous and highly respectable meeting of the inhabitants of
Ashburton and neighbourhood held at the chapel of St Lawrence,
Ashburton the 12th June 1845 to adopt such policy as may be necessary
for the formation of the above railway, it was resolved.

That it is highly desirable that this town and neighbourhood should
possess all the advantages arising from railway communication and that

* Town known just as 'Newton' at this time.

52

those advantages would be best served by the construction of a line from Ashburton to Newton (Abbot*) station of the South Devon Railway; . . .

That this meeting having heard with satisfaction the statement made by the provisional committee that the S.D.R. Co have expressed their readiness with this company do request the committee to continue their exertions to carry into effect the wishes of this meeting as expressed in the former resolution."

At a public meeting of the inhabitants of Newton and its neighbourhood held at the Globe Inn, Newton Abbot on 8th July 1845, it was proposed, "that this meeting has heard with satisfaction the statement made by Robert Tucker Esq as one of the solicitors of the Ashburton, Newton and South Devon Junction Railway Co showing the steps which have been taken by the provisional committee of the said junction railway, to ensure the formation of a railroad from Ashburton to Newton (Abbot*) station of the South Devon Railway and feeling convinced that the only line which can prove beneficial to the town and neighbourhood of Ashburton, is the proposed line from Ashburton to Newton (Abbot*) from the formation of which, great benefit will also be obtained by this town and neighbourhood. This meeting pledges itself to use its best endeavours to carry out the objects of the said provisional committee."

At a public meeting held at the Guildhall in Totnes on Friday the 14th June 1845:—Edward Luscombe Esq., the right worshipful Mayor in the chair; it was resolved unanimously: seconded by the Rev. M. Lowndes, "That it is most essential to the interest and welfare of this town and neighbourhood to be connected by railway with the towns of Buckfastleigh and Ashburton as leading to develop the resources of this important town and rich agricultural district."

On the motion of Mr. J. F. Fogwill; seconded by Mr. J. Huxham, "That this meeting accept with pleasure, the offer of the inhabitants of Buckfastleigh to cooperate in the project of connecting the town of Totnes with Buckfastleigh and Ashburton by railway and that every exertion be used to promote the undertaking."

It was not until the 27th July 1848 that the Bill for the 10½ mile line received the Royal Assent. I. K. Brunel was the engineer considered for the project and his estimate for £103,500 for a broad gauge line proved to be optimistic. The authorised capital turned out to be no less than £130,000. The first meeting of shareholders was held on the 28th September 1846, Brunel's optimism prevailed and it was stated that the line would be easy to construct despite the hilly terrain.

The South Devon Railway Co would be the operators of the line on a rental of some 4% of the capital, the Chairman of the meeting declared work would begin immediately. So much for the promise, for on the 20th June 1847 the next meeting of the shareholders took place and no

Ceremonial spade with which the first sod was turned on 3rd August 1865.

Photo: Nicholas Horne Ltd, c'ty of Totnes Borough Museum.

PRESENTED TO

Mrs. W. Hamilton

by Messrs. Branson & Murray

on the occasion of her cutting the first sod of the

BUCKFASTLEIGH TOTNES & ASHBURTON RAILWAY

on the 3rd day of August 1865.

Enlarged view of the inscription of the ceremonial spade.
Photo: Nicholas Horne Ltd, c'ty of
Totnes Borough Museum.

such start had been made! The country was in a financial crises (not new to this modern age) and the consequential cuts in public spending which followed deemed it necessary for the scheme to be delayed.

In 1849 further investigation required the project to be abandoned if the country's railway affairs did not improve considerably. By 1851 it was clear that they were indeed not improving and the Chairman of the company advised its dissolution, by now a formality.

In the meantime, the South Devon Railway under Brunel had reached Totnes on the 20th July 1847. It was to carry on eastwards to arrive at Plymouth (Laira Green) on the 5th May 1848. It was not its terminus, for this was Millbay and was not reached until the following year 1849, when the completion of Mutley tunnel was achieved.

In the building of the main line through Newton Abbot to Totnes, Ashburton and Buckfastleigh were forced into a social decline. The two towns first lost their valuable coaching trade and their distance from the new railway stations simply accelerated the decline of their important woollen and mining industries. This in time had the effect of making it impossible to attract alternative work to the area and the lack of new sources of employment led to depopulation. It was due to this fact that numerous plans were submitted for railway branch lines to connect these towns to the main line.

The passing of the years produced a continued decline of Buckfastleigh and Ashburton and their inhabitants lost faith in the future and in themselves. Finally, during 1862 these local inhabitants decided they had had enough and the decline must now stop.

They decided to go all out for a line from Totnes to Buckfastleigh where the majority of the woollen mills still survived, more in fact than did at Ashburton.

In November 1863 the plans were deposited with the Devon authorities for two railways from Totnes. Railway No 1 of 6f and 70 links in length to Totnes Quay and railway No 2 of 6m 7f 4chs in length to Buckfastleigh. Principal landowners involved included the Dukes of Somerset and Cleveland; Earl of Sandwich; Lord Cranston; Sir Walter Carew Bart., Church of England; Thomas Mitchelmore; John Barnes; John Collard; Jeffery and Thomas Edwards; and Thomas Abbot.

The following year, on 25th June 1864, the Buckfastleigh, Totnes & South Devon Railway Company was authorised by act of parliament and the first General Meeting of the shareholders of the company was held at Churchwards Hotel, Buckfastleigh on the 29th August 1864.

At a Special General Meeting of the Proprietors held at the Castle Inn, Totnes on Tuesday the 9th day of May 1865

John Bowden Esq in the Chair

The Secretary having read the Motion convening the meeting, the Chairman explained that it had been convened in pursuance of the standing orders of Parliament for the purpose of approving the Bill which had been introduced to authorise the extension of the line to the Town of Ashburton and the Solicitor having read the particular clauses to effect this object

It was moved, seconded and

Resolved

That the bill now submitted (instituted?) "a Bill for enabling the Buckfastleigh, Totnes and South Devon Railway Company to extend their Railway to Ashburton" be and the same is hereby approved of—

John Bowden
Chairman

It was on the 26th May 1865, following much consultation, the company obtained a second act of Parliament extending the line from Buckfastleigh to Ashburton. The change of heart was meant as an incentive to arouse the local inhabitants from their state of general apathy. Everybody knew the need for a railway to revitalise these two towns but few had faith enough to risk 'hard cash' investment. Little help was forthcoming from the S.D.R. which had ample expenditure to cover with its main line schemes, so it was left to a few with their investment and fund raising ventures to spell out the final success of the project.

Progress during the following years 1867 to 1870 are recorded in the extracts taken from the reports of the half yearly General Meetings:-

from Engineers Report 16th February 1867

"The line is formed and partially ballasted from Totnes to the boundary of Staverton Parish and a large quantity of earthwork and masonry has been done on the extension to Ashburton."

from Engineers Report 20th July 1867

"Station building at Buckfastleigh commenced."

8th Half Yearly General Meeting held 29th February 1868

It was stated that during the whole of the last six months negotiations were pending with the contractor under which it was hoped that he would be able to complete his contract. Although negotiations were not at an end at the time of the meeting the Directors were convinced that until "a new contractor can be procured the work must remain, as at present, at a standstill."

It also became necessary, "owing to the time allowed for the completion of the line having nearly expired, to apply to Parliament for an extension of time and a Bill for this purpose has accordingly been prepared and introduced, and has passed the Second Reading".

As there had been no progress in the works during the past six months there was no Engineers report.

9th Half Yearly General Meeting held 30th September 1868

The Directors could not report any progress with the works. An Act had been obtained extending the time for the completion of the line for a further period of two years. Measures were being taken to obtain additional subscriptions for shares.

10th Half Yearly General Meeting held 27th February 1869

The Directors reported that in the Autumn of 1868 an arrangement was entered into with Mr. Tollit to complete the unfinished portion of the works at Buckfastleigh so that ". . . on possession being obtained of the Ecclesiastical Commissioners land in Staverton, the construction of the line between Totnes and Buckfastleigh must be proceeded with uninterruptedly".

They also reported that "A fresh survey has also been made and adopted, for a deviation at Ashburton, whereby a considerable reduction in cost will be effected, and a better communication obtained between that town and the station."

12th Half Yearly General Meeting held 30th April 1870

The directors reported ". . . that the difficulties with which they have had to contend, have been surmounted, and all arrangements made for ensuring the completion of the Railway".

They also stated that "By an Act of last year the Company was empowered to assign a Preferential Dividend to 3000 of the £10 Ordinary Shares, and at the Special Meeting to be held after the termination of the General Business, the Proprietors will be asked to sanction the issue of £30,000 by means of Preference Shares of £10 each, bearing a fixed annual Dividend of five per cent per annum. A resolution will also be submitted authorising the Directors to borrow from time to time on Debentures, under the provisions of "The Buckfastleigh, Totnes and South Devon Railway Act 1864" "The Buckfastleigh, Totnes and South Devon Railway Act 1865" and "The Buckfastleigh, Totnes and South Devon Railway Act 1869" any sum or sums of money not exceeding £32,000.

13th Half Yearly General Meeting held 29th September 1870

The Directors reported that ". . . the long pending negotiations for the purchase of the property of the Ecclesiastical Commissioners had been brought to a close; these negotiations have been beyond all expectations, tedious and protracted but the settlement of price having been left to the arbitration of Mr. Sturge, of Bristol, and his award having been made, the Directors have sincere pleasure in announcing that the amount has been paid, and that

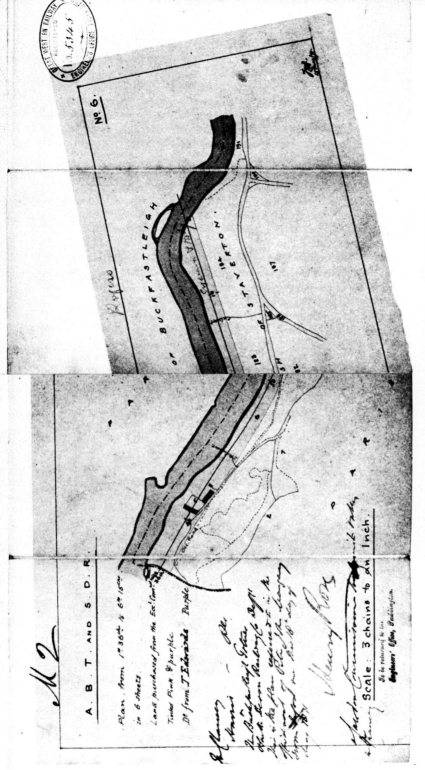

Photograph of the ends of No 6 section of the original plan for the Ashburton, Buckfastleigh, Totnes and South Devon Railway, dated 15th May 1871.

British Rail (W.R.)

the Contractor will be placed in immediate possession of a considerable portion of ground".

The station buildings at Buckfastleigh had been completed and those at Ashburton commenced.

Phase II.—Life as the Buckfastleigh, Totnes & South Devon Railway. 1872—97.

It was in April 1872 that the words "Change for the Ashburton Branch" appeared for the first time on the brightly painted notice board at Totnes station ready for the opening of the new branch line.

Finally, it was on Mayday, the 1st May 1872, that the nine miles and twenty chains of the line opened amidst much gaiety in the two towns. There were day long celebrations with some 1500 public luncheons for the ladies and the gentlemen and free teas for the poor.

The long day started at 5 a.m. with the sounding of church bells, and at Buckfastleigh, Hamlyn's brass band paraded the streets at intervals. Ashburton was decorated with ornamental arches, flags and Chinese lanterns and one high streamer bore the inscription 'May the good Lord send us prosperity!' The local press stated that—"never certainly, was there a lovelier Mayday!"

The celebrations over, the Buckfastleigh, Totnes & South Devon Rly., settled down to serving its community with four passenger trains each way, daily, but alas, these made little impact on the prosperity of either town. True, tourists appeared in small numbers but decline and decay continued at Ashburton and the passenger service did not appear to be paying its way. Luckily, this was not so of the freight service, as almost half of Devon's surviving woollen industry was centred on Buckfastleigh. In fact, for some years Buckfastleigh had provided more freight traffic to handle than had the busy market town of Newton Abbot itself.

The woollen traffic, the coal traffic to and from the mills, together with what was left of the mining traffic supplemented the poor receipts from the passenger service. However, the following extracts the 17th & 18th half yearly General Meeting reports of the company did not apparently indicate very much concern over the passenger side of the undertaking, on reporting returns and receipts for the same.

17th Half Yearly General Meeting held 28th September 1872
The Directors reported on 30th June 1872 that the line from Totnes to Ashburton was open and that the gross receipts for the two months amounted to £752 7s 7d and that after deducting the working charges of the South Devon Company a net profit of £417 17s 6d was obtained. Over 20,000 passengers and 4,000 tons of goods were carried.

60

They also reported that "To meet the requirements of the Goods Traffic, enlargements of the stations and additional siding accommodation will be required. The construction of the Railway from the Totnes Station to the Quays will also be proceeded with as soon as the final arrangements for the purchase of the land have been concluded. The Directors regard the completion of this work as essential to the ultimate success of the undertaking, since it will tend very materially to develop the Resources of the District".

18th Half Yearly General Meeting held 31 March 1873

Gross receipts for the half year ending 31 December 1872 amounted to £1893 10s 0d and the net income to be carried to the credit of the Revenue Account (assuming the statement furnished by the South Devon Company to be correct) was £1055 12s 7d. The number of passengers carried was 45,336, by far the larger proportion being third class. Goods traffic was slightly in excess of 12,000 tons.

The Directors also reported that "The work on the Tramway to the Quays at Totnes were commenced in October last, but have been considerably extended by the state of the weather during the Winter. The Contractor has been put in possession of the whole of the land, and the rails for the Permanent Way have been delivered; the completion of this essential portion of the undertaking may therefore be anticipated in the course of a short time."

The Quay line had by now been completed but had not been opened due to signalling difficulties at the junction with the main line. This was reported by the 19th half yearly meeting of the 18th October 1873:-

19th Half Yearly General Meeting held 18th October 1873

The Directors reported that "The Tramway to the Quays on the Plains has been completed for some time past, but its opening has been delayed in consequence of the Interlocking System of Signals at the junction with the South Devon Main Line not being in an equally forward state."

They also reported that ". . . it will appear that the gross receipts from passengers and goods are such as to justify the expectations originally entertained; but your Directors regret to be obliged to add that in consequence of the South Devon Company having adopted in the division of the traffic receipts, principles which your Directors are advised are not warranted either by the terms of the Agreement, or by Clearing House practise, and which certainly were not contemplated at the time the Agreement was made, the Balance placed by the

61

South Devon Company to the credit of your Company will leave nothing for Dividend. Your Directors have therefore appointed a committee to meet the South Devon officials ... that the matters in difference will be treated by both sides in a spirit of fairness and conciliation and that they will be able to announce to you ... that they have received on your behalf the due proportion of the joint purse earnings".

It was resolved at the meeting "That the Shareholders whilst placing every confidence in the Directors ... urge upon their Directors the necessity of renewed exertions on their behalf, and (unless a satisfactory arrangement be arrived at with the South Devon Directors) of taking the matter before the new Railway Tribunal."

It will be noted in the above report that concern was being shown regarding dividends to shareholders. The passenger returns were not cited as the direct cause, but rathermore the legalities of the 'division of traffic receipts' with the S.D.R. were held responsible.

The income of the independent branch line company was soon to be supplemented by goods traffic on the Quay Line, which finally opened on the 10th November 1873. This line was worked only by horses until the 24th August 1874 whereupon locomotive power was permitted to within twenty yards of the level crossing. Over the crossing and for the rest of the line, horses remained in control. This was required by act of Parliament and was not rescinded until as late as 31st May 1948 when tractor power was then employed. This is borne out in the 20th half yearly report of the company following:-

20th Half Yearly General Meeting held 21st May 1874

"Your Directors in presenting the amended accounts for the year 1873, would congratulate the Shareholders on the recent decision of the Railway Commissioners, as to the Terminal Allowances due to this Company.

The amended account shows a gross revenue for the year ending 31st December 1873, of £4147 12s 10d, and a net balance of £2127 4s 0d, the Terminal Allowances under this decision amounting to £1327 4s 0d for the year. The full benefit of this decision however, will not accrue to the Company until the returns of the present year are completed; insomuch as a large portion of the Terminal Allowance had, in these accounts to be made good from the mileage receipts of both Companies.

Your Directors would call attention to the great benefit to the Company, as also to the Trade of Totnes which would arise from a more frequent use of the Tramway to the Quay by the traders of the district; and great care should be taken by consignees to book their goods to and from Totnes Quay, in order that the

Company may obtain the advantages of the full rate, and Terminal Allowances, which they are not entitled to on goods sent to Totnes Station."

It was also reported that the South Devon Company had recently applied to Parliament ". . . for leave to substitute Steam for Horse-power over that portion of the railway which connects the Totnes Station to the Quays". The application was only partially successful because the Board of Trade objected to an engine crossing the street on a level and so the use of an engine was authorised to within twenty yards of the Road.

22nd and 23rd Half Yearly General Meetings held 11 September 1875

The South Devon Company had obtained powers from Parliament to work locomotives over the Quay Branch. The Directors again made reminder that as much traffic as possible should be sent over the Quay Branch.

The continuing struggle for trade and improvements sought for the company for both lines, progressed vigorously through the early 1870s. The struggle was an uphill one and the writing was soon 'on the wall' for it having ultimately to go into liquidation. The fact that the S.D.R. was transferred to the G.W.R. during 1876, the latter company had taken over responsibility for working the Buckfastleigh railway as agents of the former. A statement to this effect was contained in the 25th half yearly report of the company, viz:-

25th Half Yearly General Meeting held 14th October 1876

"In consequence of the transfer of the South Devon Railway to the Great Western Company, the latter Company has since the 1st of February 1876 worked the Buckfastleigh Railway as agents for the South Devon Company."

The Buckfastleigh, Totnes and South Devon Railway Co., continued to exist as an independent company through the 1880s. Its fortunes however did not improve and by 1896 moves were afoot to put the company into liquidation. By August 1897 a liquidator was appointed following Royal assent to an Act of Parliament to transfer the company's assets to the Great Western Railway Co. This was duly done following with the G.W.R. taking over the Ashburton and Totnes Quay branches as from 28th August 1897. Reference is made to the above in extracts from three Special Meetings of the two companies during 1896—7 as follows.-

Special General Meeting held 31st August 1896

It was resolved "That the Agreement for the amalgamation of the Buckfastleigh, Totnes and South Devon Railway with the Great Western Railway dated the 10th August 1896 now submitted to this meeting be and is hereby approved."

The branch during the early part of this century.

A general view of Totnes station in 1912, looking eastwards and showing the old S.D.R. atmospheric pumping station behind the 'up' line buildings.

L. & G.R.P.

Looking eastwards from Totnes station in 1913, showing Ashburton Junction signal box, just behind the water crane. The goods shed can be seen to the right of the picture.

L. & G.R.P.

Totnes station exterior in 1913, viewed on the 'down' side, showing the original signal box.

L. & G.R.P.

A '655' class, 0-6-0PT No 1747, with a goods train during shunting operations on the 'up' through line. Date not known but thought to be early 1920s.

Staverton station captured during the early 1900s, looking towards Totnes.

R.C. Sambourne collection.

A train for Totnes leaving Buckfastleigh, hauled by a '517' class 0-4-2T during the summer of 1906. Note the four wheeled coaching stock.

Chapman & Son.

(a) Ashburton terminus viewed from the road during the early 1900s. A '517' tank stands with a train from Totnes alongside the coal supplies for future trips.

J. L. Smith collection, c'ty O.P.Co.

(b) View from the end of the platform after the engine had run around its train for the return journey.

J. L. Smith collection, c'ty O.P.Co.

An unusual view of Ashburton station in the early 1900s, showing the forecourt and roadside advertisements. Note the gleam on the engine's dome!

L. & G.R.P.

S. D. R.

Passenger's Luggage.

Ashburton to

Churston

It was resolved "That the Bill now submitted to the meeting instituted 'A bill for conferring further powers upon the Great Western Railway Company in respect of their own undertaking and upon that Company . . . for amalgamating the Buckfastleigh, Totnes and South Devon . . . with the Great Western Railway Company and for other purposes' be and the same is hereby approved subject to such alternation therein as may be sanctioned by Parliament".

At a special General Meeting held on 23rd August 1897 a liquidator was appointed as the Royal Assent had been given to the Act of Parliament for the Transfer of the Property and Undertakings of the Buckfastleigh, Totnes and South Devon Railway Company to the Great Western Railway Company.

At a special General Meeting held on 30th December 1897 the Buckfastleigh, Totnes and South Devon Railway Company (In Liquidation) was told that the holders of Ordinary Shares would be paid £3 5s 0d per share out of the £22,450 which the GWR had agreed to pay for this purpose and that ". . . the balance of this amount as well as any balance which might remain to the credit of the Capital and Revenue Accounts after discharging all the costs and expenses of and incidental to the winding up, and of all debts and liabilities of the Buckfastleigh Company should be paid to the Directors as compensation for unpaid services extending over a period of nearly 30 years". The Preference Shares and Debentures were to be exchanged for GWR stock in accordance with the terms of the Agreement for Amalgamation.

During this traumatic period, the lines were also to change their gauge. They were originally built on the Brunel 7' 0¼" broad gauge and on the momentous weekend of the 21/22 May 1892, were converted with much of the rest of the Westcountry, to the now standard gauge of 4' 8½". On 23rd May three standard gauge trains ran down from Exeter and commenced the first full passenger service on the branch following the change.

Phase III.—Life as G.W.R. Branches, 1897 to 1948

There is little of great impact to record covering the next 50 years in the lives of these two lines, save for the proposed link up of the railways in South Devon during the period known as the 'silly season'. Plans were deposited with the Devon Authorities during 1898 for a so-called Brent, Ashburton & Heathfield (Mid Devon) Railway.

The act called for two railways to be constructed, railway No 1 running from a junction with the Teign Valley line, crossing the Moretonhampstead branch to Ashburton, a total length of 7m 3f 7c 75lks. Railway No 2 running from Ashburton via Buckfastleigh to join the main line at Brent, a total length of 7m 6f 19chs. Needless to say, this useless project of pure duplication was never carried out and all that remains of the scheme are the deposited plans now residing in the Devon County Records Office, Exeter.

This is not the end of the story, for in November 1899 plans were again deposited with the Devon Authorities, this time for no less than four further railways in the South Hams area of Devon.

They were as follows, the well known extension of the then new Yealmpton branch opened in 1898, to Kingsbridge via Modbury, a total length of 12½ miles, a shorter spur from Kingsbridge to Salcombe of just 3 miles; a 15 mile stretch of line from a junction with the Torbay branch, just above Kingswear, crossing the river Dart to Dartmouth and on to Torcross and Kingsbridge; a fourth, 6 mile stretch of line from this same junction on the Torbay branch to run up the west bank of the river Dart joining on to the Totnes Quay line itself. The South Hams would really have been 'opened up' in terms of development if this all had taken place as the map shows!

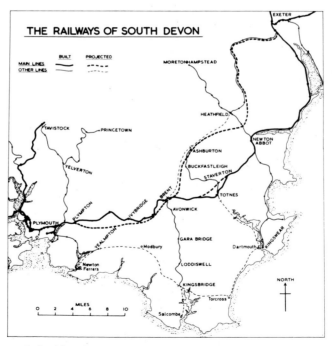

A map of the 'South Hams' showing the proposed railways in addition to those that came to fruition.

R. E. Taylor

Staverton station looking towards Buckfastleigh in 1921. Note the cyder barrels on the platform.

L. & G.R.P.

A general view of Ashburton station on a glorious 1st of June, 1921.

L. & G.R.P.

An 0-4-2T No 4870, sets back on to the 'up' platform road with auto coach No 96, ready for another journey down the branch on 30th August 1945.   H. C. Casserley

Ashburton station during the Great Western days of August 1945. No. 4870 and an auto coach await for departure to Totnes.

H. C. Casserley.

Under the ownership of the G.W.R. the freight remained good and the passenger service began to improve. This was due to the good publicity being given to the line by the G.W.R., i.e. by encouragement rather than necessity. In 1906 the steam railcar was introduced on the branch in order to give a more frequent service at cheaper cost. Unfortunately, they were not a great success and they later gave way to the more familiar push and pull auto train used extensively on Great Western branch lines throughout the system. However, these two branches gave sterling service to their communities through the early half of this century with their peak around the 1910 era.

As already stated, there is little other to record in the history of the branches prior to their nationalisation, both world wars promoted an increase of activity on the branches due to the respective war efforts. During the 1920s and onwards passenger traffic began to decline generally with the advent of the motor car. This, coupled with the fact the bulk of passengers required to travel to and from Newton Abbot rather than Totnes accelerated the decline accordingly. The G.W.R. augmented the service again in 1930 but the results were disappointing. Ashburton people still travelled by road to Newton Abbot and the branch was used almost exclusively by people on strictly local journeys, including those employed at the Staverton Joinery Works. By the late 'thirties the car was here to stay and as the road traffic increased from Ashburton over the 7 miles to Newton Abbot so the passenger traffic decreased proportionately over the 18 rail miles between the two towns. The line was in a decline and closure was only prevented by virtue of its beauty as a tourist attraction, coupled with the fact no through bus service was available from Totnes to Ashburton. The fact responsible for this was the boundary of the areas served by the Western National and the Devon General bus companies passed between the two towns.

The Quay line on the other hand still continued to give service to the light industry on its route to the bank of the river Dart. The steam traction ended near the level crossing and was taken over by Clydesdale horses, owned and operated by the Blight family, from the crossing to the quay itself. Following the second world war, the Great Western Railway had but two years existence left, for the then Socialist Government under Attlee had but one remedy for all the ills of industry—nationalisation! Successive governments are still trying to make it work, but nevertheless, it was on the 1st January 1948 that the two branches came under new ownership once again, this time the Western Region of British Railways. Little change was forthcoming for time was running out fast for both lines, one sooner than the other.

TO BE REPLACED BY MECHANICAL POWER

For many years horses have pulled their loads across the level-crossing in Totnes main street from the timber and cider yards to the railway sidings. Yesterday they transported their last consignment —seen in the picture—for they are being replaced by tractors.

One of the rare photographs of the horse drawn traffic on Totnes Plains. The photograph, off a newspaper copy, shows the last day of horse drawn operation on 31st May 1948.   Western Morning News, c'ty of
Nicholas Horne Ltd.

Phase IV.–Life under British Railways. 1948 to 1962

This phase as it applied to the Ashburton branch, was the shortest and saddest of all. There is little to recount, save for the obvious, the woollen and mining industries which were once the life blood of the line had long since vanished leaving only cattle and timber plus a little quarry-stone.

The deepening inroads of motor traffic sapped the last of the passengers from the line, a pattern that had now become nationwide. The branch thus declined still further and was forced into closure some four years before the odious broom of Dr Beeching swept away the vast majority of the Westcountry railway system altogether.

It was on 1st November 1958 that the branch saw its heaviest passenger traffic for some time,–it was also its last day of operation. Goods traffic, now mainly cattle, carried on at the rate of five trains per week each way, but even this traffic was diminishing. It is interesting to note that further passenger trains, other than 'farewell specials' did run on the line from 1958 until complete closure in 1962. These were annual Sunday School Outing trains running from Buckfastleigh to Teignmouth, and back. A combined Sunday School Outing for children, teachers and parents took place on the last Wednesday in June each year from 1958 until 1961, and again on Wednesday 1st August 1962, even though one assumes that the line was down-graded to goods traffic standards during this latter period.

The inevitable last goods train ran on Friday 7th September 1962, hauled by 2–6–2T No 4555. On the following day the Plymouth Railway Circle ran a farewell trip hauled by another 2–6–2T No 4567. The Ashburton branch was therefore closed to all traffic on and from the 10th September 1962, just over 90 years after its joyous and optimistic opening. The Quay line continued to run a goods service of sorts for a further three years after this date, closing on 14th June 1965 excepting for the private sidings off it. The private sidings were to continue to be served until 4th December 1967 by B.R.

N.B. Photographs of the Sunday School Outing trains in 1959 and 1960 appear on pages 119 and 120 respectively.

No. 7 3 4   (2304/1)

BRITISH RAILWAYS (WESTERN REGION).

TRAIN STAFF TICKET.

ASHBURTON BRANCH

Train No............................   **(UP.)**

To the Engine-driver.

You are authorised, after seeing the Train Staff for the Section, to proceed from BUCKFASTLEIGH to TOTNES, and the Train Staff will follow.

Signature of Person in Charge.................................

Date...

Noisy funeral for Dart Valley Railway

FIREWORKS AND THUNDER

TO the accompaniment of fog signals, fireworks, whistles, and thunder and lightning the last passenger train on the Dart Valley branch line made noisy, but slow progress between Totnes and Ashburton on Saturday night.

It carried about 700 passengers including many local people who admitted they had never travelled on the line before, and also railway enthusiasts from as far away as London and Birmingham.

Earlier in the day hundreds of enthusiasts had taken photographs of the trains all of which starting with the mid-day trip from Totnes consisted of five carriages and two locomotives instead of the usual one or two coaches.

Such indeed, has been the interest in the demise of the picturesque line that Mr. L.R. Dinwiddy, the stationmaster at Buckfastleigh, received between 200 and 300 letters from people in other parts of the country asking for a ticket between any two stations which they could keep as a memento.

Councillor-driver

Many people elected to say their goodbye during daylight so that they could obtain a last glimpse of the railway's view of the River Dart, but it was, of course, the last train which attracted the chief attention. The locomotives were Nos. 1466 and 1470, and one of them was driven by a member of Ashburton Urban Council, Mr. W. Cartwright.

Ashburton was particularly well represented, as the passengers included the chairman and the Clerk of the Urban Council, Mr. Alan French and Mrs. G. Morris, and also the Portreeve and the Bailiff, Mr. C.J. Harris and Mr. H.W. Brockway. None of the other places on the line was officially represented.

After an elaborate shunting movement at Totnes the last train left almost on time at 6.45 to the cheers of a small crowd. At once the fog signals and fireworks began to explode and nature contributed to the noise and flashed by producing a short thunderstorm.

Hundreds of people were gathered by the side of the line to see the train pass. Many houses had every room fully lit and all the curtains drawn back for the occasion.

Top-hatted mourner

The train being longer than the platform two stops were necessary at both the intermediate stations—Staverton and Buckfastleigh—where one of the mourners came dressed in a silk top-hat.

The younger passengers imitated the tuneful whistle conversations being held between the two engines; older ones spoke of bygone days, when the railway regularly carried heavy traffic. Slogans in chalk appeared on the windows.

Meanwhile, a crowd several hundred strong had formed at Ashburton and when the train came noisily to a standstill the platform was probably thronged with more people than ever before in its history—except on May Day, 1872 when the town welcomed its first train as the wonder of the age.

With railwaymen being photographed and interviewed as though they were film stars, there was inevitable delay before shunting manoeuvres began again.

Some tears

In any case, some passengers who wanted to alight were not able to do so because of the crowds on the platform, while others who wanted to join the train found it almost impossible to drive a way through the mass.

But eventually the two squat little tank engines backed their five coaches clear of the crossover and ran round the loop line to join the other end of the train. This movement had to be performed carefully, as the loop line is only just long enough to take five coaches.

Officially the era was already over, but as British Railways might have some other use for the rolling stock, an unofficial return trip had to be run, and passengers were allowed to use it. About 250 did so.

The departure from Ashburton was again accompanied by fireworks and cheering —and even by tears from one or two people, who evidently loved the branch line so dearly that they found the general tenor of the funeral distasteful.

No 'Auld Lang Syne'

But there was no "Auld Lang Syne," and, though he was wearing his chain of office, the Portreeve did not follow the example of his predecessor of 1892 who draped in black crepe the last broad gauge locomotive to leave the town before the conversion of the gauge.

On the return trip two stops were again necessary at Buckfastleigh and Staverton, while at Totnes the unofficial train arrived simultaneously with both up and down local ones on the main line giving the station staff one of their busiest moments ever.

One goods train each way will continue to run to Ashburton on Mondays to Fridays, at least for the time being, and bus services are being increased along the route. It is not yet known whether British Railways intends to continue running race specials to Buckfastleigh or the annual Buckfastleigh Sunday schools outing train.

Western Morning News 3rd Nov. 1958.

G.W.R.

Ashburton

G. W. R.

TOTNES

Phase V.—a) Ashburton Branch: Dereliction and rebirth as the Dart Valley Railway, 1962 to 1975.
  — b) Quay Line: Demise to Lifting. Birth of the Great Western Society Ltd. en passant, 1962 to 1969.

Author's Note:

During the early 1960s, the histories of the Ashburton and Quay lines became perhaps more complex and interdependent than during their conception some ninety years before.

Much has been written and said about both the Dart Valley Railway and the Great Western Society since that time, but nowhere is recorded the heartaches, disappointments, intrigues, suspicions and all the many trials and tribulations ascribed to the setting up of these two fine and noble Westcountry institutions.

I therefore make no apologies to readers for the lengthy detail of the histories of these two bodies which consituted most of the fifth phases of the histories of the two lines.

I feel too many people, including members of both bodies, take for granted the fruits borne of the traumatic and enigmatic years of the setting up of such as the D.V.L.R. and the G.W.S.

I was privileged to serve on both committees during these trying years. As such, I organised and supervised the first joint working parties of enthusiast labour at Buckfastleigh on two very cold and wintry week ends of 20th November and 5th December 1965, producing over 40 volunteers on each occasion. On these grounds alone, I submit my qualification to comment in detail within the following narrative.

Finally, readers may be confused regarding the ownership of 0-6-0PT No 1369 referred to later. Initially it was purchased with the aid of a private fund supervised by a quorum of joint D.V.R/G.W.S. members and was handed over to the G.W.S. on the Quay line where it ran on public open days. When it became apparent that the two bodies were to develop in their own distinctive ways, the two principal fund raisers, fearing the locomotive would move out of the Westcountry, negotiated its transfer to the D.V.R. The two remaining custodians of the fund, not wishing to create animosity, did not oppose the move. This was approved by the Management Council of the G.W.S. following which, any G.W.S. member wishing to sell out his shares to the D.V.R. could do so. No 1369 being already at Buckfastleigh to make way for Burton Agnes Hall on the Quay line, stayed there on the subsequent removal of G.W.S. stock in· December 1967. It has remained there ever since.

78

The first intimation to the public that the Ashburton branch might not be demolished but reopen, appeared in the *Western Morning News* on the 20th September 1962, a copy of which appears below.

PLAN TO REOPEN ASHBURTON LINE

DURING the last few months a group of 14 professional and business men have been working on a plan to reopen the Ashburton branch line—recently closed even to freight traffic—as a holiday attraction.

Many of the details have been worked out, and negotiations have been taking place with the Western Region headquarters at Paddington. A definite proposal is likely to be made this autumn.

The scheme has considerable financial backing, but whether or not it succeeds still largely depends on the attitude of the Western Region. The big question is whether the Region will be prepared to lease the line on a rental basis, at least for the first few years, or whether it will offer only outright purchase or nothing.

In theory British Railways welcome the idea of enthusiasts taking over abandoned section of track. The Bluebell Society now profitably operates (during the summer only) a nine-mile section of a Sussex branch line which shortly before its closure carried only 35 passengers daily.

OUTRIGHT PURCHASE

In practice, however, some officials dislike the idea of enthusiasts succeeding where professional railwaymen have failed—albeit in entirely different circumstances. Thus, while Paddington could appear to welcome the scheme, it could prevent it by insisting on outright purchase—for a sum, probably between £50,000 and £75,000.

If the professional and business men can win a lease, all would seem to be plain sailing. A non-profit-making company would be formed to take over the railway; members would have to guarantee funds sufficient to make good any losses, but this would not cause difficulty. Under the umbrella of this company, actual operation of the railway would be carried out by a voluntary society, which might perhaps obtain a Light Railway Order under an Act of 1896.

A very small permanent staff might be employed, but most work should be done voluntarily by railway enthusiasts, of which there are no lack in South Devon in the summer.

At least until it had proved itself reliable, the new management would not be permitted to take trains into British Railways' station at Totnes, and this would necessitate building a new platform just before the Ashburton branch joins the main line. (The Bluebell Society has now completed its apprenticeship and is allowed to share British Railways' station at Horsted Keynes.)

NEW STATION

Another new station would be built at Dart Bridge, Buckfastleigh, to reduce the walking distance to the Abbey. Ashburton would be regarded as the headquarters station and a museum of G.W.R. locomotives and rolling stock would probably be established.

Trains would, of course, be steam hauled, and initially two locomotives of the 1400 class would probably be bought—perhaps at £600 apiece. Passengers would mainly travel in "auto-cars", the open-seating vehicles which used to be employed on the Saltash pull-and-push trains before the advent of Diesel units.

A service would probably operate between June and September on most days of the week, with perhaps special trains at Easter and Whit week-ends. A timetable would be published and adhered to, so that once more it would be possible for holiday-makers to Ashburton to complete their journey by train.

DART VALLEY

It would be hoped that through travel arrangements could be made with British Railways, coach companies, and the River Dart Steamship Company. The railway—sometimes known as the Dart Valley line—offers fine views of the lower fresh-water parts of the river.

For a long time railway enthusiasts have felt that there is room for a voluntarily-run steampowered branch railway in the West country. About two years ago several of the professional and business men involved in the present venture systematically surveyed all branch lines between Westbury and Truro to discover which might suit their needs best.

The short Brixham branch and the more ambitious Looe line were obvious possibilities, because their trains do not have to share mainline platforms at the junction stations. Brixham, however, gave too little scope. At present British Railways have no plans to close the line to Looe, and even if goods traffic ceased to go to Looe itself, clay might still be handled at Moorswater. Moreover, in the Beeching era the future of the main line through Liskeard is sufficiently uncertain to worry the enthusiasts.

ADVANTAGES

The final selection, there, was the Ashburton branch, now closed completely, but in a fair state of repair. There are obvious advantages. South Devon's holiday trade is growing more rapidly than that of any part of Britain.

Towns at both ends of the line attract large numbers of sightseers, while the railway passes close to Buckfast Abbey. There are sufficient sidings at Ashburton to house some of the locomotives and rolling stock already bought by individuals—Ashburton may yet welcome one of the G.W.R.'s giant "Castles," though, of course not in steam.

All this is not merely an enthusiast's dream. The solicitors (no fewer than four), surveyors, chemists and engineers who have worked out the preliminary details have been careful to avoid premature publicity, and even now they are not ready to receive offers from would-be part-time engine drivers, guards and stationmasters.

At present all that is required is further guarantee. If and when the time comes for other help, there is no doubt that it will be forthcoming—as there is no doubt that Ashburton and other Councils will give the venture their support.

Western Morning News, 20th September, 1962.

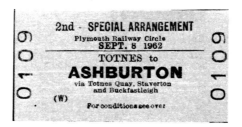

An upline view of Ashburton during the 'waiting years', 1964.

R. C. Sambourne

244

C. R.

TO

Buckfast-leigh

(85)

S. D. R.

Passenger's Luggage.

Staverton to

Lidford

(96)

S. D. R.

Passenger's Luggage.

Staverton to

KINGSWEAR

Staverton station viewed during the 'years of waiting', 1964.

R. C. Riley.

(a)

(b)

(c)

Scenes at Buckfastleigh during the long days between closure and re-opening as the Dart Valley Railway. (a) Looking towards the station, (b) Looking towards Ashburton from the platform, (c) as in (b) but taken from the signal box. This section is now lifted.

R.C. Sambourne.

To appreciate the emergence of the Dart Valley Railway as we know it today, one must examine more closely the origins, intentions and aspirations of the principal pieces of an involved 'chess game' played during the early 1960s. The line, it was stated was to be opened by a group of fourteen professional and businessmen. These gentlemen had conceived the idea of an independent railway operating as a G.W.R. line as far back as 1957–8, prior to closure to passenger traffic by British Railways.

On 6th May 1963, the *Western Morning News* again reported on the affair. It stated "The railway enthusiasts bid for the branch line is not a leap in the dark, but the culmination of several years of study." It went on to say "A figure of well over £100,000 which has been in circulation, refers to the Moretonhampstead branch: the South Devon Railway Society was formed especially with the view to taking over the Moretonhampstead branch line, but has now abandoned the plan and is supporting the Ashburton effort." *The Western Independent* took up the story next and reported in its issue of 17th November 1963, "Many different lines had been suggested for preservation earlier". It reiterated the statement made by the *Western Morning News* regarding the S.D.R. Society's proposals and went on to mention several other possibilities in Cornwall. It also reported certain essential points regarding the Ashburton branch viz:- "The fourteen sponsors would form a non profit making holding company which would buy the line (at a capital cost estimated at between £30,000 and £40,000: B.R. would not lease), while a voluntary society would provide much of the materials and labour as well as the day-to-day enthusiasm to run it profitably." The line had been disused for about 18 months at this time.

Further reports were to follow in quick succession as most of the local newspapers and the media took up the story. Rumours were rife, wild speculation sprung up as to whom the mysterious businessmen were and all but the 'Mafia' were named as possibilities!

However, the 'secret' was out on the 13th June 1964 when the *Western Morning News* gave a comprehensive report on 'Devon's Bluebell Line'. Nine of the gentlemen behind the project were named;

Mr. P. Sutcliff. (A trustee of Dartington Hall.)

Mr. R. J. Saunders. (Civil Engineer of Staverton Contractors.)

Mr. A. Morgan. (Chartered Surveyor.)

Mr. J. M. Bowers. (Solicitor.)

Mr. P. J. Garland. (Chartered Accountant; Treasurer of the Tal y Llyn Rly.)

Mr. P. B. Whitehouse. (Managing Director and Treasurer of the Tal y Llyn Rly.)

Brig. Sir Ralph Rayner.

Mr. C. F. Ricketts.

Mr. K. A. Davis.

The author, standing on the platform, organises one of the working party groups present at Buckfastleigh on 20th November 1965.

P. F. Bowles

Collett '22XX class' No 3205 undergoing restoration at Buckfastleigh during 1966, before its transfer to the Severn Valley Railway.

R. C. Sambourne

A resplendent scene at Ashburton station during the brief D.V.L.R. era of restoration. No 1420 simmers gently on the summer afternoon of 20th July 1970.

J. M. Boyes

No. 4555 receives a last minute cleaning prior to Members day on 3rd April 1971. Ashburton station existed then in its fully restored condition.

C.G. Lennox-Jones

No. 1420 waiting to leave with the 11.30 a.m. train for Totnes on 23rd May 1970.

J. M. Boyes

A now historic picture showing the northern end of Buckfastleigh station confines. It pictures the permanent way train for the relaying of the loop line at Staverton, returning on completion of the event, 23rd May 1970.

J. M. Boyes

No 1420 passes by Buckfastleigh signal box during shunting operations on 18th July 1970.

J. M. Boyes

The Coat of Arms of the Dart Valley Railway is made up of the Arms of the Cities of London & Bristol, (G.W.R.) and the Arms of the Towns of Totnes and Ashburton.

The newspaper went on to report on a meeting between a firm of solicitors acting for the D.V.R. and the Devon Roads Committee at Exeter the previous day. It confirmed enthusiasts fears that the section of line between Buckfastleigh and Ashburton should not reopen as it was required for road improvements. The County Surveyor, Mr. Henry Creswell, was quoted as saying "If the line were closed it would facilitate improvements to the A38. If not it would cost £60,000 more for other improvements."

The Chairman, Mr. A. C. Shobrook, said the Buckfastleigh to Ashburton stretch should be lost to the company. (Agreement was later reached however to lease this stretch from British Railways until the said road improvements were actually to take place.)

It was to be six and a half years before the line was to reopen again and from 1962—67 the negotiations and objections dragged on. The main tasks confronting the businessmen were to register the Dart Valley Railway as a company and to transfer the line from British Railways ownership to that of the private company. It was some considerable time since anyone invoked the various light railway acts and consequently the authorities concerned were out of touch and much time was wasted. However, sufficient progress was made by the 2nd October 1965 to allow a joint train made up of Dart Valley and Great Western Society members stock to move up to Buckfastleigh, the first train since 1962.

It is interesting to note that a support body of enthusiasts, formerly called the Dart Valley Railway Association, was inaugurated on the 22nd October 1966. This was suitably celebrated by a special train running to Ashburton, the first passenger carrying train since 1958. Finally, on Saturday, 5th April 1969, the Dart Valley Railway was opened and the first public passenger train ran to Ashburton. It consisted of 0-6-0PT No 6412, a pair of auto-coaches at each end, carrying 300 passengers and left Buckfastleigh at 11.15 a.m. This was the culmination of many years of hard work, the light railway order was signed the previous Tuesday, 1st April and came into operation the following day. This legalised the purchase of the line as far as milepost 7, opposite Buckfastleigh signal box, the rest of the line being on lease.

It was not until the 21st May 1969 when Lord Beeching performed the official opening ceremony, making in the process, the rhetorical statement "If I had not closed this branch, I could not now be opening it!"—Well done Dr. Beeching, I feel history might have recorded a more appropriate person performing this all important ceremony.

Despite its problems, the Dart Valley Railway progressed from strength to strength during the years 1970 to 1975 and at the time of writing, all seems set for a great future. The latest and most important venture of the Company is the long awaited construction of the new station at 'Totnes Riverside'. A report by Mr. Taylor from the D.V.R.A. magazine 'Bulliver' follows:-

With the decision to run only as far as Staverton next season, we have been granted absolute occupation of the section between ¼m.p. and ½m.p. for a period of 18 months subject only to passing certain special workings and maintaining run-round facilities as far as possible. This means that we can now progress with the building of the main station and development of the whole site with a decent chance of getting it into a reasonable condition before the grand re-opening in 1977. The restriction of having to work between service trains, with all its attendant problems, will no longer arise.

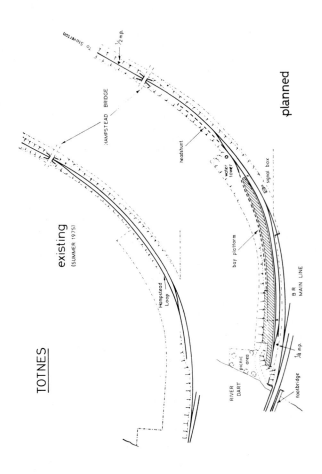

As can be seen from the accompanying plans, the track layout will change considerably from that we have known since Hampstead loop was built in 1970. Currently, a local plant hire firm is completing the earthworks, but as we are now progressing with the complete development of the site, extra fill will have to be brought in during the coming months. The existing fill is being used to build up land adjacent to the main line, and the present loop will then be extended as shown. Most of the existing Hampstead loop will be re-covered and used in the new layout, which will avoid having to re-lay it to passenger standards. These initial changes are shown by the solid lines on the second diagram; the dotted lines indicate proposals for future development. Once the trackwork and filling is complete, the first section of platform between the points marked "x" will be built. The building of the headshunt on the site of the old loop, the bay, extension of the river end of the platform and the station buildings will depend very much on finance and on enthusiast help.

(Editor's note: All plans so far published for Totnes are subject to the scrutiny and approval of the D.o.E.).

The only sad and depressing item to report during this period was the inevitable loss of the 2½ mile stretch from Buckfastleigh to Ashburton. With this went the station buildings, goods shed, engine shed and many valuable trackside items and sidings. Gone also were the rural surroundings which encompassed Buckfastleigh station, replaced by a new dominant structure, that of the high level precast concrete monstrosity of a flyover. It strides across the valley in a strangely menacing manner, commanding the skyline in the direction of the town like something from a space odyssey. The sound of the car and heavy lorry pounding its surface, finally and persistently rupturing the quiet peace that had reigned here for so long. It was on 2nd October 1971, the last trains* ran to the historic stannary town of Ashburton and during the following month the contractors moved in to dismantle the track in order to convert much of the trackbed to roadway.

The railway to Ashburton has finally gone, the 'Railway Hotel' is now renamed 'The Silent Whistle'; the old malthouse is occupied by a firm of manufacturers, F. J. Bacon Ltd but the final 'salt' in the railway 'wound' is the fact that the old engine shed is now a workshop for Davey & Williams, Motor Engineers, as is the old Brunel station building occupied by Jack Riley, another Motor engineer, who has converted it into a garage and filling station. Yet another round to the infamous car!

---

* Including through trains from London and South Wales.

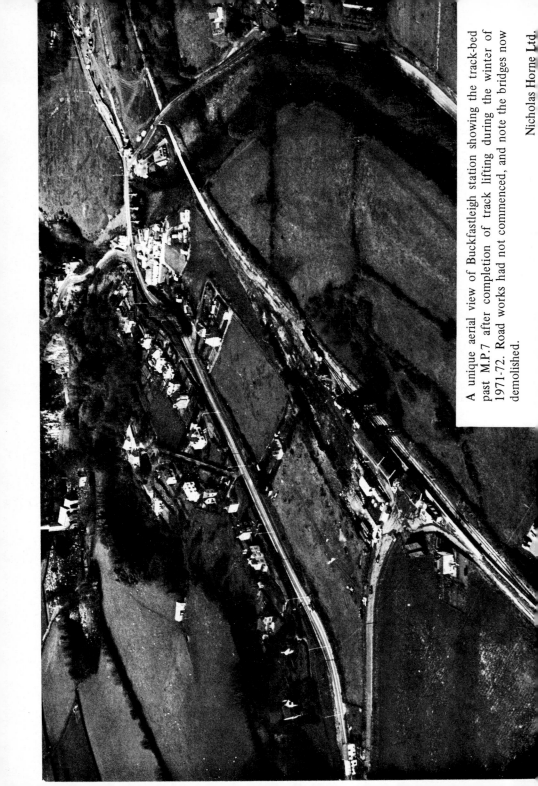

A unique aerial view of Buckfastleigh station showing the track-bed past M.P. 7 after completion of track lifting during the winter of 1971-72. Road works had not commenced, and note the bridges now demolished.

Nicholas Horne Ltd.

Phase V.—b) The Quay Line 1962 to 1969.

During the years of the conception and birth of the Dart Valley Railway after the closure of the Ashburton branch in 1962, its partner the Quay line, was to remain open and in addition provide the setting for a very different but unique scene. British Railways were to operate a goods service on the line until 14th June 1965 and as late as 4th December 1967 for Private sidings off it. Stavertons, South Devon Farmers, the grain merchants, together with the cattle market, built in more recent years for the then Totnes Borough Council, were still using the goods service of the line until 1967. Further along the line however, the Harris bacon factory and at the end of the branch, Reeves timber importers, had turned over to road transport during 1964—5.

Here, on this somewhat lowly goods line was to develop the virtual rebirth of the Great Western Railway only sixteen years after its demise. Here, in this backwater of light industry in the little market of Totnes was to form the nucleus of an enthusiast company, limited by guarantee, of the Great Western Society Limited.

To comprehend this company, the other principal 'piece in the chess game' referred to earlier, one must digress slightly from the Ashburton and Totnes Quay lines. One has to move to Southall, Middlesex during 1961, for it was here that summer that a group of young men got together to form the 48XX Preservation Society. Their sole aim was to preserve an 0-4-2T of the 14XX class, and an auto coach to run on a privately owned line somewhere. Later that year, with a membership of 30, the society aims were extended to cover interest in the whole of the G.W.R. and the name was changed to the Great Western Preservation Society.

In 1962 an inaugural meeting was held to formulate the precise aims and objectives of the new G.W.P.S. This done, the society commenced to make itself known in the railway world and it launched its magazine, 'The G.W. Echo'. By 1963 membership was only 150—not very encouraging, so it was with a third change in name, to the Great Western Society, they tried again! Hopes blossomed into reality and by 1964 membership rose to over 500. During the year, the fund launched to purchase 0-4-2T No 1466 also materialised and this is where we return to Totnes for the continuation of the story.

The search for a home to run No 1466 and her auto coach coincided with the setting up of the Dart Valley Railway project and negotiation with this body resulted in the idea being born for the G.W.S. to represent railway enthusiasts on the railway. To this end, the need for temporary storage for No 1466 and her coach was required and further negotiation with the then Totnes Borough Council secured a loan of their little used cattle market sidings off the Quay line. So with due ceremony on the 18th March 1964, No 1466 arrived down the Quay line to these very sidings. Working parties set about the restoration whilst the purchase of a suitable auto coach was sought. However, on 12th June that year, quite a different kind of coach arrived, a 1905 vintage 'Dreadnought'. This had been purchased by a member and presented to the Society. Meanwhile a member was pursuing the idea of preserving the 0-6-0ST from Millbay Docks, Plymouth, No 1363 which had already been withdrawn and was languishing in the round-house at Laira. This was duly achieved by way of a private fund and on the 27th August the same year 1363, by now presented to the Society, arrived on the Quay line to join the other two items.

The Management Council were quite excited at the success of the Society and decided to hold its first open day to the public. This was held on the 17th October 1964 when history was made by the running of the passenger train on the Quay line! Both engines responded well and the hopes of the most optimistic organiser were exceeded when the expected 150 visitors planned for topped the 400 mark. The year ended just as successfully as the long awaited auto coach arrived in late December—it was No W231W.

By now it was 'unofficial public knowledge' that the Dart Valley Railway on the Ashburton branch and the Great Western Society on the Quay line were part and parcel of the same venture and enthusiasts on both sides worked with that understanding.

The following year 1965, turned out to be a momentous one for both parties, the D.V.L.R. itself being officially formed on the 25th June. It was much earlier in the year when the curious public, that continually turned up to see people from all walks of life working on some very old and dirty engines on the Quay line, were confronted with yet another arrival! On Saturday, 20th February, G.W.R. 0-6-0PT No 1369 made its last 61¼ mile run under British Railways ownership from Wadebridge to Totnes, arriving in great style in front of T.V. cameras and local press. Mr. P. A. Lemar, the Society's local representative formally received the engine from Mr. W. H. Needle, the Totnes station master and the scene was punctuated with the mellow whistle of No 1363 which was in steam alongside. It was in fact steamed to celebrate the inauguration of the formation of the South West Group of the Society of which Mr. Lemar became the first Chairman. A 'members open day' was held on the 26th June and No 1466 and her auto coach ran for the first time in private hands. On August 19th 1965, the entire membership of the South Devon Railway Society were absorbed into the G.W.S. (S.W. Group), in true Great Western style.

Further excitement occurred during the October of 1965; firstly on the 2nd, locomotives No 3205, managed by Mr. D. Rouse and No 4555, owned by Mr. P. Whitehouse, worked an Ian Allan special from Exeter to Totnes. On being uncoupled from the special they worked some privately owned coaches to Buckfastleigh for storage and future use on the line. (No 3205 was subsequently removed to the Severn Valley Railway when Mr. Rouse left Devon.) This was followed on the 9th with another very successful open day for the G.W.S. on the Quay line when No 1369 was steamed and coupled to the auto coach, giving rides to the public.

It was not until the 2nd April 1966 that the Quay line was to make history again. It was then to have running upon it for the first time, a full sized G.W.R. 4–6–0 tender engine in the form of No 6998, 'Burton Agnes Hall', the Society's new acquisition.

Having worked a steam special the previous day around the Oxford area, this engine was sent to Devon for storage at Buckfastleigh. However, due to complications in respect of the light railway order for the Dart Valley, this engine could not go down the branch to Buckfastleigh and was relegated to the Quay line. To make room, the G.W.S. moved No 1369 to Buckfastleigh during the previous night and then, similarly, moved No 1466 and auto coach No 231 soon after No 6998 arrived on the following day.

The following June of that year, G.W.S. newsletter No 12, had this to say to its members regarding No 6998, "Members may have been surprised to see some of the Society stock has moved down the branch to Buckfastleigh in early April and since this coincided with the ballot regarding the future of stock, it is fit that an explanation is due. It was realised soon after buying the 'Hall' that, with the ending of steam in the London Division planned for early April, No 6998 would be soon trapped at Oxford and have to travel 'dead' to a Society depot. After due consideration it was decided to send it to Devon for temporary storage at Buckfastleigh ..."

The ballot referred to in this newsletter was the subject of an A.G.M. on the 19th February 1966, when the G.W.S. Management were to ask its members to vote them a clear mandate for action. This action authorised them to decide whether the G.W.S. Council was going to 'go in' with the D.V.L.R. exchanging stock for shares, or 'pull out' and go its own way. To this end, a comprehensive document, GWS/DVR I, dated 26/3/66 and agreed by both parties, were sent to Society members stating the whole position entailing the legalities of the association with the D.V.L.R. These were duly considered, but because the D.V.L.R. required ownership of G.W.S. stock, and had anyway formed the Dart Valley Association, it was decided to withdraw and remain independent.

During these tense and anxious months, the Society depot continued life with numerous 'members open days' on the Quay line. (The remainder of their stock remaining static at Buckfastleigh).

On May 13th 1967, a joint open day was organised between the G.W.S. and the D.V.L.R. but alas, British Railways refused permission to allow any steaming at Buckfastleigh on the grounds it was still legally their line! To offset the disappointment to the public, No 6998 was quickly prepared and steamed at Totnes, giving footplate rides to visitors coming down from the static display at Buckfastleigh.

During the following September, the G.W.S. Ltd issued a progress report on the negotiations concerning the D.V.L.R. and the result of the ballot the previous March, it read as follows:-

Progress Report issued jointly by Great Western Society Ltd. and Great Western Preservations Ltd. — September, 1967.

A long time has elapsed since Members were given news of the Society's progress towards an ultimate goal. News of the individual locomotives and rolling stock has been circulated from time to time, but little else has been said since the interim report of negotiations with the Dart Valley Light Railway was made in February, 1966. It is quite understandable therefore that some member may have been critical of us and wondered what is happening. It can only be said that since that report we have been actively pursuing possibilities other than total involvement with the Dart Valley Company. They could not, because of their delicate nature, be openly discussed, or our objectives could have been prejudiced. However, matters have now been brought to the point where there would appear to be nothing preventing our reporting on progress so far.

Dart Valley Light Railway

Early negotiations with the originators of the DVLR were most cordial and we are indebted to these people who gave us storage for our first items of stock and a basis on which to expand the Society. The prospect of a union between this Society, representing as it does a large number of Great Western enthusiasts voluntarily submitting to reasonable discipline in the pursuit of their interests, and a company operating an attractive branch line, were excellent. However, changes of influence amongst the Dart Valley promotors resulted in the formation of a separate body giving direct support to the Dart Valley Company — namely the Dart Valley Association, formed on 22nd October 1966. Our relations with this body are good.

The ballot of members, in March, 1966, authorised us to conclude negotiations for the Great Western Society's involvement with the DV project if we thought fit. Because the DV Company would not be looking to the Society for direct support, we thought it best for other possibilities to be explored. 1466 and the Auto-coach have not, therefore, been passed over to the DV company, nor has any other stock. Should it appear best for them to go over, and for 6998 to go to the Dart Valley Museum (the original intention), this would not be done without an agreement in writing that we would be allowed to run 6998 at least for a limited distance, on the branch at reasonable intervals. An open mind is being kept on our future with the DVLR,

96

but at present the likelihood of future participation with them appears to be partial rather than total.

Unfortunately, this news nurtured gloom and despondency amongst local enthusiasts, many of whom had joint membership anyway.

1967 was not a good year for either side, the D.V.L.R. were still bogged down with negotiations on the Ashburton line and notice had been served to the G.W.S. by British Railways of the impending closure of the Quay to all goods traffic. The provisional date for the closure was given as the 4th December, with January 1968 as a possible date for lifting. To try to alleviate the depression, an 'open day' to the public was organised, albeit for the last time, for October 21st 1967 and both No 6998 and 1363 were steamed and gave the usual footplate rides to visitors. Again it was a very successful day with hundreds of people turning up to see the spectacle. Unfortunately the bulk weight of a 'Hall class' engine was too much for the line and a fishplate broke in half in cattle market sidings which restrained the activity of No 6998 during the late afternoon.

The following month, G.W.S. newsletter No 19 had this to report on the current situation:–

Stock Movement

"Further to the recent progress report (September, 1967) it has been decided by the Council of the Great Western Society Ltd. and the Board of Directors of Great Western Preservations Ltd. that should the opportunity of moving items of stock now stabled in Devon arise this would be done. After a meeting with B.R. representatives on November 11, 1967 and due to the forthcoming closure of the Totnes Quay Branch and the wish of the Dart Valley organisation for a settlement of their affairs in Devon, an opportunity was given for the movement to take place. It has, therefore, been decided that locomotives 1466 and 6998 and coaches W231W, 3299 and 5952 will be moved from Devon on December 2, 1967 in steam on the condition that tests and trials carried out between now and then are successful. The stock is to be moved during the next two weeks to Plymouth Laira MPD for turning and the movement on December 2, will commence from there. Because of only three weeks' notice of the movement, it is impossible at present to give timings. Locomotive 1363, because of its mechanical condition, is not able to be moved from Devon. The Hawksworth coach, 7372 purchased by the South West Group is to remain in Devon due to outstanding loans. The future of 1369 is as yet uncertain. A break with the Dart Valley project has therefore been made and the aims of the Society and Preservations companies are now centred upon a steam museum at Didcot and the possible running on the Wallingford branch."

This was then to be the parting of the ways and on November 25th the Society stock moved from Buckfastleigh to join items on the Quay line where it was to be assembled for a journey to Laira, Plymouth for servicing and turning the engines. On Sunday November 26th 1967, the cavalcade of partly restored locomotives and stock of a wide range of vintage, reversed out of the Quay line for the last time en route to Laira. On Saturday December 2nd this same train passed through Totnes within sight of the former depot on its way to the new Society home, that of the M.P.D. at Didcot, Berks. (now Oxon). The sole occupant of this otherwise deserted branch was the little 1910 vintage dock shunter, No 1363 looking sadly dejected. It had been decided that this engine be retained in the Westcountry and as such was destined to stay on the Quay branch for over a year whilst the South West Group of the G.W.S. negotiated a new home for it at Bodmin, Cornwall.

Despite the delays in vacating the branch, it closed to traffic as predicted on the 4th December 1967. Lifting however, was not to commence until No 1363 had finally left. This final break with Totnes occurred when, in sheer defiance, the Quay line made further railway history on the 1st May 1969. 'Warship' class diesel D809 "Champion" entered the line fighting against strong opposition from undergrowth to tow No 1363 out 'dead' to the main line. Its driving rods removed, it started its journey from Totnes to St. Blazey, Cornwall that night, still being towed by the 'Warship'. The two engines were to participate at the British Rail open day at St. Blazey the following Saturday. (It was later transferred to its subsequent location, at the erstwhile G.W.S. depot at Bodmin).

Thus ended a unique and colourful era for the Totnes Quay line. Now deserted, it was soon truncated from the main line and lifting proper was commenced by Thomas Ward & Son in early Autumn of that year. The lifting of track as far as the level crossing was completed by 7th December 1969, beyond that point, the rails initially remained in situ, as did a 30 ton weighbridge some 100 yards beyond the crossing. Most of the rails were soon at least partially covered by tarmac, but outside the warehouses of Messrs Reeves Ltd they remained exposed and firmly set in concrete, albeit often covered with large quantities of imported timber unloaded from continental ships plying the river Dart. (N.B. Photographs of the vestiges of the old Totnes Quay Line appear on pages 152, 157 & 158).

Final words from each side on the old D.V.L.R./G.W.S. alliance were:–
G.W.S. Newsletter No 20, dated December 1967 which stated "...........
DART VALLEY RAILWAY Newsletter No 19 through being produced very hastily contained only a brief mention of our policy regarding the Dart Valley project, this we now propose to clarify. It has become obvious to the Council over the past two years that the Dart Valley project has little to offer the Membership of the Great Western Society. As most of the Society's Stock has been preserved through the donations of many hundreds of members, we believe that these members

should be given the opportunity of actively participating in the restoration, and possible operation of the Society's Stock. The Council
therefore acting on the mandate given to them by the Membership
during the early part of 1966 decided that a withdrawal from the Dart
Valley project should be made. Accommodation at present being provided at Didcot M.P.D. is better, and more adequate than that hitherto
provided by the Dart Valley. We would like however, to take this
opportunity of expressing our sincere thanks to the Dart Valley
organisation for the provision of storage facilities afforded to us during
the past few years. Also we would like to wish them every success
during the coming years, and look forward to their opening next year."

D.V.L.R. magazine, 'Bulliver' dated January 1970 – The Editor stated:–
"The D.V.L.R. is not a preservation society. It has no need to be when
the G.W.S. is so well equipped to collect and preserve Great Western
history and stock. Our organisation serves a complimentary purpose, to
help maintain and operate a short railway in Great Western fashion..."
    I as author will heartily echo these sentiments.

No 1466 and auto coach W231W giving rides to visitors during G.W.S. 'open day' on 26th June 1965.

G.W.S.

No 1369 and auto coach W231W taking over the visitor trade during the G.W.S. 'open day' of the 9th October 1965.

G.W.S.

Railway history being made. A 4–6–0 'Hall' class, No 6998 enters the Quay line on 2nd April 1966 under G.W.S. ownership.

A.R.K.

The author stands partially obscured by steam from No 6998, *Burton Agnes Hall* as it struggles to fill its tender from Mill Leat. This incident was in preparation for the 'open day' of 17th May 1967.

G.W.S.

The heaviest concentration of motive power ever to amass on the Quay line. A 4–6–0 tender engine and three tank engines take part in an early morning preparation for the departure of the G.W.S. to Didcot. 26th November 1967

P. A. Lemar

The final day of the G.W.S. depot on the Quay line. No's 6998 and 1466 prepare to leave with their train for the last time on the 26th November 1967

A.R.K.

The first privately owned engine to run on the Quay line. G.W.S. owned 0-4-2T, No 1466 in Stavertons yard during April 1964, shortly after delivery by B.R.

P. A. Lemar

The very last railway engine to use the Quay line. G.W.S. owned 0-6-0ST No 1363 waits in solitude for a new home to be found during the spring of 1969.

A.R.K.

TIME TABLES AND BRANCH WORKING

Branch Workings

Broad Gauge
Originally worked by S.D.R. 0-6-0, *'Tarus'* – purchased by the Co in 1869. G.W.R. B.G. No 2170; later converted to standard gauge and renumbered 1326.

1876 onwards
- 6 wheeled, 3 compartment Dean coaches.
- after the absorption of the S.D.R. Armstrong 2-4-0ST's as Avonside conversions of 1877.
- *'Melling'* was known to have been in collision at Buckfastleigh in 1892, and *'Cerberus'* is believed to have been shedded at Ashburton during the early 1890's.

Other possibilities are any of the eight 0-6-0ST's goods engines of the S.D.R., later G.W.R. No's 2143-4; 2148-53, the last *'Argo'* was withdrawn 1892. Any of Armstrongs 0-6-0 general purpose engines of both broad and standard gauge eras e.g. 1228-1237; 1243-1257; 1561-1580.

Standard Gauge
After 1892 through to the 1920s – various types of the '517' class 0-4-2 Tanks, e.g. 1163.

1906
- 4 wheeled, standard gauge Dean coaches.
- Excursions – Dean Clerestory stock.

1920s   Steam railcars introduced.

Mid 1930s to late 1950s
- 0-6-0PT's of the '655' & '2021' classes. e.g. 2116.
- 0-4-2 Tanks of the 48/58XX class, later 14XX class. e.g. 1427; 1429; 1439; 1466 & 1470.
- Auto trailers No's 55; 130; 192; 196; 229 & 231.
- B. R. days 'B' set non-corridor stock, i.e. Non Cord 2nd + Non Cord 2nd brake.
- Goods locos 2-6-2 Tanks of the 44XX and 45XX classes. e.g. No's 4405 & 4555. (On occasions, passengers). 5569.

104

Trains of Note:–

1.11.58	Last passenger train hauled by 0–4–2T's 1470 & 1466 (6 coaches).
24.6.59	Sunday School Special, hauled by 2–6–2T's 4561 & 5573 (8 coaches).
29.6.60	Sunday School Special, hauled by 2–6–2T's 4561 & 4555.
28.6.61	Sunday School Special, as for 1960 but only on the branch: No 4975 'Umberslade Hall' employed on the main line to Teignmouth and back to Totnes.
1.8.62	Sunday School Special, hauled by 2–6–2T's 4567 & 4574, but only on the branch: No 5003 'Lulworth Castle' employed on the main line workings.
7.9.62	Last goods train ex Tavistock Junc., hauled by 2–6–2T 4555.
8.9.62	Plymouth Railway Circle Special, hauled by 2–6–2T 4567.
2.10.65	G.W.S./D.V.R. members special hauled by 2–6–2T 4555 & 0–6–0 3205.
2.4.66	G.W.S. special stock movement, loco 0–4–2T 1466. Auto coach W231W plus private coaches.
22.10.66	Formation of the D.V.R.A. special, hauled by 2–6–2T 4555. Ran two trains of 3 auto coaches each.
5.4.69	D.V.L.R. opening train, 0–6–0PT 6412 & two pairs of auto coaches.
21.5.69	D.V.R. opening ceremony, directors special, *'Master Printer'*, hauled by 0–6–0PT6435 and 2–6–2T 4555 (6 coaches).
2.10.71	Two D.V.R.A. specials from Totnes (BR) to Ashburton and back. Part of the 'last trains to Ashburton' celebrations, hauled by 2–6–2T 4588 (8 coaches). Second train hauled by 0–6–0PT 6435 and 0–6–0PT 1638.
6.5.72	Branch Centenary Specials – 2 ran, both hauled by 2–6–2T's 4555 & 4588 (6 coaches).

Quay Line –

Great Western Society Stock:–

> 0–4–2T No. 1466*
> 0–6–0ST No. 1363
> 0–6–0PT No. 1369*
> 4–6–0 No. 6998, *'Burton Agnes Hall'*
> 1905, 70' 'Dreadnought' coach No W3299.
> 1951 Auto coach No W231W*

Buckfastleigh:–

> 1948 Hawksworth coach, 1st/3rd Brake compo, No W7372.
> 1935 Collett Coach, all 3rd, No W5952.
> During 4/66 items marked * shifted from Quay line to here.

DART VALLEY RAILWAY

STOCKLIST OF PRESERVED VEHICLES as at 13th February, 1971

LOCOMOTIVES—Steam

CLASS	NO.	CODE	WHEELS	DESCRIPTION	DESIGNER	BUILT	NOTES
*Ind'l	2031	–	0-4-0 ST	Industrial Shunter	Peckett & Sn.	1942	ex-Exeter Gas Wks. (B7)
1366	1369	U U	0-6-0 PT	Weymouth Dock Tank	Collett	2/34	Outside cylinders (B2)
48XX	1420	U U	0-4-2 T	Auto-Train Tank	Collett	11/33	Monogram
48XX	1450	U U	0-4-2 T	Auto-Train Tank	Collett	7/35	
16XX	1638	A Y	0-6-0 PT	Pannier Tank	Hawksworth	3/51	Dart Valley (B1,7)
45XX	4555	C Y	2-6-2 T	Prairie Tank	Churchward	9/24	Great Western
45XX	4588	C Y	2-6-2 T	Prairie Tank	Churchward		
64XX	6412	A Y	0-6-0 PT	Auto-Train Pannier	Collett	11/34	
64XX	6430	A Y	0-6-0 PT	tanks with small	Collett	3/37	
64XX	6435	A Y	0-6-0 PT	wheels.	Collett	4/37	Monogram
*Manor	7827	D B	4-6-0	"Lydham Manor"	Collett	12/50	(B4,6)

LOCOMOTIVES—Diesel

CLASS	NO.	CODE	WHEELS	DESCRIPTION	DESIGNER	BUILT	NOTES
Shunter	D2192		0-6-0	204 H.P. Shunter	Gardiner/Drewry	1961	Swindon built (B3)

GOODS VEHICLES

CLASS	DESCRIPTION	DESIGNER		NOTES
S65494	Covered goods van	12T XP		Ex-S.R.
125814	Covered goods van	12T STD		Mink
42223	Covered goods van	14T EP		DAMO B
*68777	Goods brake van	20T		Toad
59119	Covered goods van	10T		Iron Mink
41873	Shunters' Truck			GWR
601	Crane	15 cwt.		GWR
4492	Petrol Tank	14T		Shell
	PW Trolley			
C19	Open Wagon	10T		PLA

COACHES

No.	COACH LOT No.	DESCRIPTION	DIAGRAM	DESIGNER	BUILT	NOTES
225	1736	Auto-trailer	A. 38	Hawksworth	25/8/51	
228	1736	Auto-trailer	A. 38	Hawksworth	25/8/51	
232	1736	Auto-trailer	A. 38	Hawksworth	25/8/51	
238	1766	Auto-trailer	A. 43	Hawksworth	25/9/34	
240	1766	Auto-trailer	A. 43	Hawksworth	25/9/34	
1285	1575	(Excursion coach—	C. 74	Collett	17/4/37	Square Decor
1295	1575	(open third	C. 74	Collett	17/4/37	Square Decor
4046	30149	Open second corridor	—	—	1954	Swindon Built (B.R.)
4166	30171	Open second corridor	—	—	1954	York Built (B.R.)
7377	1690	Corridor, Brake compo.	E. 164	Hawksworth	25/12/48	Ex Royal Train
*9111	1471	Super Saloon "King George"	G. 60	Collett	1/11/31	DVRA Club Room
9116	1471	Super Saloon "Duchess of York"	G. 60	Collett	7/5/32	DVR Co. Board Room

PULLMAN SALOONS

No.	COACH LOT No.	DESCRIPTION	DIAGRAM	DESIGNER	BUILT	NOTES
13	113	"DEVON BELLE" Observation Car	J	R. Levin	1918	Ex-LNWR ambulance car Finally Sc280M (B2,5)

ENGINEERING SALOONS

No.	COACH LOT No.	DESCRIPTION	DIAGRAM	DESIGNER	BUILT	NOTES
7	Wg. 293	Dynamometer Car	—	Churchward	16/3/01	Royal Clerestory Now cafeteria car.
*215	(944 (conv	Mess Van 4-Wheeler Lot 1560 ex-Newton Abbot Breakdown train	U. 4	Dean	15/504	Originally 1st/2nd Ex-6008, ex-747 (B2)
80971	804	Newport Eng. Saloon	G. 31	Dean	17/10/96	Clerestory Roof ex-8231, ex-9035
80977	1170	Gloucester Eng. Saloon	Q. 1	Churchward	13/8/10	Ex-6479. Rebuild as Inspection Saloon
80978	745	Plymouth Eng. Saloon GWR Director's Saloon	G. 3	Dean	27/10/94	Royal Clerestory Ex-8249, ex-9045

GOODS TRAFFIC ON THE BRANCH, TAKEN AT ITS ZENITH.

Incoming Traffic

ASHBURTON
Coal — Domestic and loco coal for the engine shed.
Animal feeding stuffs/Farm seed/Fertilizer.

BUCKFASTLEIGH.
Coal — Domestic/Commercial for the mills, electricity and gas depots.
Wool/Sheepskin/Hides — from all over the Westcountry and Oxford area.
Farm machinery/Ironwork/pig iron — for the foundry.
Wood pulp/sulphite/clay/resin — for the paper making industry.
Sand and Timber — from the Quay line.
Whitsuns only — Racehorses.

STAVERTON
Meal/Grain
Timber — for the joinery works
In addition to the above there were the usual 'pick-up goods' of a general type at all three stations. All traffic differed during the passing of time and the above represents a good cross section during the lines zenith.
General input of coal was 20 - 25 wagons per week.
General goods traffic was in the region of 40 wagons per day.
Racehorse traffic was at the rate of 60+ horses per meeting.

Outgoing Traffic

ASHBURTON
Umber — for paint manufacturing
Malt — from Tuckers maltworks.
Milk/Rabbits.
Cattle — outgoing from the 4 cattle fairs per year.

BUCKFASTLEIGH
Wool/serge — mainly despatched to Bradford area.
Quarrystone — arrived at station in steam lorries.
Pelts/Leather
Timber
Paper/Newsprint/Wrapping paper — from paper mills
Cattle/Milk/Rabbits — market trade.
Apples — to the Quay for cyder.
Seed.

108

STAVERTON

Cyder — from Hills factory.

Furniture etc., — from Stavertons mills and joinery works.

As for the incoming traffic, there were the 'station truck' despatches of general goods.

General output of coal empties was 20 — 25 wagons per week.

General output of goods wagons was 20 — 25 wagons per day.

Cattle trucks from Ashburton fairs were 70 or more per fair.

Horse box traffic were in the region of 10 — 20 trucks per meeting.

Note:— During the second world war, the American Army had a massive stores complex at Buckfastleigh catering for approximately a ¼ million men. There was also a number of 'buffer depots', the storage of food supplies for an emergency during wartime, set up by the Government at Buckfastleigh. Heavy traffic for both of these items were additional to the branch during this time but of course, details are not available.

QUAY LINE GOODS TRAFFIC, TAKEN AT ITS ZENITH.

Incoming Traffic

Sand — dredged from the river Dart and brought to Totnes by barge.

Trees — for Reeves timber yards.

Grain/seed — Holmans warehouses.

Apples — for Symmonds cyder works. (Old Chapel).

Pigs — for Harris bacon factory.

Outgoing Traffic

Timber — from Reeves timber yards.

Cyder — from Symmonds works.

Bacon — from Harris factory.

General goods traffic on branch at its zenith was approx 30 wagons per day. In more recent years there were building supplies and engineering goods to Stavertons Works and animal feeding stuffs, grain etc., to South Devon Farmers.

During the second world war, the old racecourse was used for the building of wooden bottomed boats for the war effort and supplies for this industry were carried on the line.

Public and Working Time Tables 1872 – 1958

UP TRAINS		1872 until further notice							
	A.M.	A.M.	A.M.	A.M.	P.M.	P.M.	P.M.	P.M.	P.M.
Ashburton dep.	7.20		9.20	11.20		2.50		4.20	7.10
Buckfastleigh "	7.28		9.28	12.00		2.58		4.28	7.18
Staverton "	7.38		9.38	12.20		3.08		4.38	7.28
Totnes arr.	7.48		9.48	12.30		3.18		4.48	7.38

DOWN TRAINS								
Totnes dep.		8.40		10.20	1.20	3.40		5.40	8.50
Staverton "		8.50		10.30	1.40	3.50		5.50	9.00
Buckfastleigh "		9.00		10.40	2.00	4.00		6.00	9.10
Ashburton arr.		9.08		10.48	2.10	4.08		6.08	9.18

June, 1890 until further notice

TOTNES QUAY BRANCH

BUCKFASTLEIGH AND ASHBURTON BRANCH.

BRIXHAM BRANCH.

110

ASHBURTON BRANCH.

Single Line worked by South Devon Block Telegraph Instruments and Train Staff and Ticket. The Staff Stations are Ashburton Junction, Buckfastleigh and Ashburton. Staverton is an intermediate Block Post.
The Crossing Station is Ashburton Junction.
When absolutely necessary two Goods Trains, or a Passenger and a Goods Train, may cross at Buckfastleigh and Ashburton on the understanding that the Passenger Train is always kept on the Running Line, and if the Passenger Train has to stop at Buckfastleigh, it must stop at the Platform.

WEEK DAYS ONLY.

Distance M C	DOWN TRAINS.	Station No.	Ruling Gradient 1 in	Time Allowances for ordinary Freight Trains See page 2. Point to Point Times.	Allow for Stop.	Allow for Start.	1 B Pass. dep.	2	3 B Pass. dep.	4	5	6 X N'ton Abbot Goods. arr.	dep	7	8 B Pass. dep	9	10 B Pass. dep.	11 B Pass. dep.	12 B Pass. dep.	13	14 B Pass dep.	15	16	17
				Mins.	Mins.	Mins	A.M.		A.M.			A.M.	P.M.		P.M.		P.M.	P.M.	P.M.		P.M.			
— —	Totnes	2001	—	—	—	1	8 40		10 35	..		10 53	12 15		12 50		3 0	4 20	6 50		8 25			..
0 17	Ashburton Junction	2000	—	—	—	—	CS		CS	..		CS			CS		CS	CS	CS		CS			....
2 58	Staverton Crossing ..	2099	—	—	—	—																		....
3 25	Staverton	2100	536 R.	8	1	1	8 48		10 43	..		12 25	12 40		12 58		3 8	4 28	6 58		8 33			....
6 75	Buckfastleigh	2101	110 R.	8	1	1	8 57		10 52	..		12 50	1 35		1 7		X 3 17	X 4 37	7 7		8 42			....
9 37	Ashburton	2102	60 R.	8	1	—	9 3		10 58	..		1 45			1 13		3 23	4 43	7 13		8 48			....

WEEK DAYS ONLY.

UP TRAINS.	Ruling Gradient 1 in	Time Allowances for ordinary Freight Trains See page 2. Point to Point Times.	Allow for Stop.	Allow for Start.	1 B Pass. dep.	2	3 B Pass. dep.	4	5	6 B Pass. dep.	7	8 B Pass. dep.	9	10 X N'ton A'bot Goods. arr.	dep.	11	12 B Pass. dep.	13 B Pass. dep.	14 B Pass. dep.	15	16	17	18
		Mins.	Mins.	Mins	A.M.		A.M.			A.M.		P.M.		P.M.	P.M.		P.M.	P.M.	P.M.				
Ashburton	—	—	—	1	7 45		9 20			11 47		2 12			2 35		3 42	5 42	7 42				..
Buckfastleigh	60 F.	8	1	1	7 51	...	9 26	....		11 53	...	2 19		2 45	x 4 40		3 48	5 48	7 48	...			..
Staverton	118 F.	8	1	1	8 1	...	9 36	....		12 3	...	2 28		4 50	5 10		3 58	5 58	7 58	...		....	..
Staverton Crossing ..	—	—	—	—	CS		CS			CS		CS			CS		CS	CS	CS			....	..
Ashburton Junction ..	—	—	—	—																			
Totnes	536 F.	8	1	—	8 8		9 43	....		12 10		2 35		5 20	5 50		4 5	6 5	8 5				..

TOTNES QUAY BRANCH.

STATIONS	Station No.	1 X Goods. arr.	dep.	2 G Engine. arr.	dep.	3	4	5		STATIONS		1 G Engine. arr.	dep.	2 X Goods. arr.	dep.	3	4	5
		A.M.	A.M.	P.M.	P.M.							A.M.	A.M.	P.M.	P.M			
Totnes	2001		7 45		4 30	....	..	...		Tram Gate			8 15		4 55	....	..	..
Tram Gate	2002	8 5		4 35		....	..	...		Totnes		8 25		5 0		....	..	..

A '517' class, 0–4–2T No 1163 and auto coach No 130 await the 'off' for Ashburton from Totnes station. Date not known, probably early 1930s.
O.P.Co.

South Devon Railway 2-4-0ST *'Cerberus'* at Newton Abbot in 1890s. This locomotive is believed to have been stationed at Ashburton near this time.

The late J.B.N. Ashford

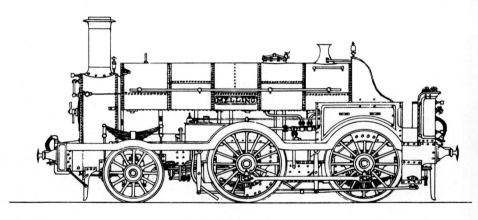

GREAT WESTERN RAILWAY ~ Broad Gauge
"Melling"

Designed by Mr J. Armstrong (17 × 24") Chimney, buffers, & Steam,
(originally as a tank engine (60") with Sanding & Bolitto Automatic
but all these are converted) ———— Vacuum Brake by Mr W. Dean.
to saddle tank engines. Engines of this type. Built at Swindon 1866.
This type engine Roberta Pollux Stewart. Weight 36 Tons in
has run the S.D.R. working order.
Launceston Branch Bury. Cerberus. Beyer. wheel base 15'.6".
Since GWR amalgamation Penn. Ostrich. Melling.
also Torquay Falmouth Hedley.
ashburton etc.

112

D46
WEEKDAYS — TOTNES AND ASHBURTON

The speed of Trains over the Branch must not exceed 40 miles per hour.
SINGLE LINE, worked by Train Staff and only one engine in steam, or two coupled together, at a time.

		H			Ruling Gradient 1 in	G	H
DOWN	Ruling Gradient 1 in	8.55 am Newton Abbot	**UP**			LE	To Newton Abbot
		7416					7320
Mileage		SX				SX	SX
M · C		am				am	PM
— · —	TOTNES .... arr	— 9 41	ASHBURTON .... dep	—		11 40	1 30
	... ... dep	10 5	Buckfastleigh ... ... arr	60 F		..	1 40
3 · 25	Staverton .... arr	536 R 10 15	.... dep			..	2 18
	... ... dep	10 25	Staverton ... ... arr	50 F		..	2 28
6 · 73	Buckfastleigh .... arr	50 R 10 35	.... dep			..	2 45
	... ... dep	11 5	TOTNES ... ... arr	536 F		12 5	2 55
9 · 37	ASHBURTON .... arr	60 R 11 15	.... dep			..	3 27

TOTNES QUAY BRANCH—Worked by Bank Engines, as required.

0–4–2T No 1427 prepares for the 'off' to Totnes from Ashburton Station.

R. S. Carpenter

Last Passenger Time Table. From 15th September, 1958 U.F.N.

D43

WEEKDAYS — TOTNES AND ASHBURTON

SINGLE LINE—Worked by Train Staff and only one engine in steam, or two coupled together, at a time.
The speed of all trains over the Branch must not exceed 40 miles per hour.

DOWN

Mile Post Mileage M	C	Ruling Gradient 1 in	Station	B Motor Rail am	B Motor Rail am	B Motor Rail SO am	B Motor Rail SO am	B SX PM	B Motor Rail SO PM	B Motor Rail SO PM	B Motor Rail PM	B Motor Rail PM	B Motor Rail PM
1	56	536R	TOTNES ... dep	7 40	8 50	10 38	11 45	12 18	12 55	2 0	3 25	4 55	6 45
2	25	536<	Staverton Crossing ...										
3	73	50R	Staverton ...	7 50	8 58	10 46	11 53	12 26	1 3	2 8	3 33	5 11	6 53
6	37	60R	Buckfastleigh ...	7 58	9 6	10 54	12 1	12 34	1 11	2 16	3 41	5 11	7 7
9			ASHBURTON ... arr	8 4	9 12	11 0	12 7	12 40	1 17	2 22	3 47	5 17	7 7

Note (7.40 am train): "To leave from Down Platform at Totnes and not to convey passengers as from that point."

Note (11.45 am train): "Not Advertised"

WEEKDAYS — ASHBURTON AND TOTNES

UP

Ruling Gradient 1 in	Station	B Motor Rail am	B Motor Rail am	B Motor Rail am	B Motor Rail SO am	G LE	B Motor Rail SO PM	B Motor Rail SO PM	B Motor Rail SO PM	B Motor Rail PM	B Motor Rail PM
60F	ASHBURTON ... dep	7 10	8 19	9 25	11 15		12 15	1 25	2 45	4 15	5 45
50F	Buckfastleigh ...	7 16	8 25	9 31	11 21	11|40	12 21	1 31	2 51	4 21	5 52
536F	Staverton ...	7 25	8 34	9 40	11c30		12 29	1 39	3c0	4c30	6c1
536F	Staverton Crossing ...										
	TOTNES ... arr	7 31	8 40	9 46	11 36	12|5	12 35	1 45	3 6	4 36	6 7

Note (G LE train, SX): "To work 12.16 p.m. from Totnes."

Rail Replacement Bus Time Table

WEEKDAYS ONLY

					Sch	V	NS			Sch	V	NS						Sch	V			NS	NS				NS	
...tion Road (Baldwin's Gar.)	...dep	...	...	...	1219	...	...		3 59	...	...		**Higher Westonfields** ...dep			Sch	V		NS	NS		NS			
(Plains)	,,	8 55	1023	1135	1220	1 20	1 45	2 20	4 04	05	3 56	5	Totnes (Plains) ,,	9 29	2 1030 1142 1227	1 30	1 30	1 52	2 27	4 7	5 42	6 12
...Westonfields	...arr	9 0 1028 1140	1225	1225	1 25	1 50	2 54	5 4	5 5	5 40	6 10	Coronation Road (Baldwin's Gar.) ...arr	9 8	9 7 9 1035 1147 1232	1 35	1 35	1 57	2 32	4 12	5 47	6 17

Sch—Operated on school Days only. V—Operated during school Vacations only. NS—Not Saturdays.

THROUGH FARE : Totnes (Plains)—Higher Westonfields ... 3d. Single

WEEKDAYS ONLY

						S			Thro' Fares from Totnes (Plains)								S				Thro' Fares from Ashburton	
									Single	Return											Single	Return
(Plains) ...dep		...	...	1145	...	...		**Ashburton (Bull Ring)** ...dep	6 55	8 10	...	1 45	...	5 50		8d	—
...(Railway Station) ,,	6 10	7 37	...	1147	4 5	5 5	...	**9d**	**—**	Buckfastleigh (Railway Station) ,,	7 5	8 20	...	1 55	4 37	6 0		1/4	2/4
...on (Railway Station) ,,			...	1159	4 17	5 17	...	**1/4**	**2/6**	Staverton (Railway Station) ,,	7 23	8 38	...	2 13	...	6 18		1/7	2/10
...leigh (Railway Station) ,,	6 30	7 57	...	1217	4 35	5 35	...	**1/8**	**2/11**	Totnes (Railway Station) ,,	7 35	8 50	...	2 25	5 3	6 30		1/8	2/11
...ton (Bull Ring) ...arr	6 40	8 7	...	1227	—	5 45	...			Totnes (Plains) ...arr	—	8 52	...	2 27	—	6 32			

S—Saturdays only.

The Rail Replacement service provided by Western National was for the benefit of employees at the Joinery Works near Staverton Station (note the mid-day Saturday journey for the half-day finish) and for school children travelling to and from Totnes.

The first and last journeys, and the Saturday mid-day journeys were withdrawn in 1970: the two surviving journeys, which by then were 'schooldays only', were withdrawn after operation in October, 1975.

A G.W.S. owned, No 1466 is 'borrowed' back by B.R. for shunting operations on Staverton's sidings off the Quay line. The engine happened to be in steam for testing that particular day in 1965.

P. A. Lemar

The station staff ranged alongside 0-6-0PT No 2116 at Buckfastleigh during 1920.

L. R. Dinwiddy.

STATION STAFFING (Taken at the time of the 1920s)

ASHBURTON
Stationmaster — 1
Drivers — 2
Firemen — 2
Guards — 2 (withdrawn after
    introduction of auto coaches.)
Carriage cleaner — 1
Porter/Signalmen — 2
Goods clerk — 1
Goods porter — 1
Length gang — 1 ganger + 4 men.

BUCKFASTLEIGH
Stationmaster — 1
Signalmen — 2
Porters — 3 (one goods)
Clerk — 1
Clerks, (Lads) — 2

STAVERTON
Stationmaster — 1
Porter/Signalmen — 2
Porter (Lad) — 1
Length gang — 1 ganger + 4 men.

Staverton Station Staff 1921.
Left to Right L. Napper (Lad Porter), Mr Barlett (Station Master), F. Baker (Signalman).

C'ty Mary Riddel.

G.W.R. Milnes — Daimler bus No 43 (Registration No T490) at Paignton station on the 17th April 1905. This was the opening day of the Paignton to Totnes bus route by the G.W.R.

H. Pitts collection

G.W.R., Maudsley bus No 202 (Registration No T3594) employed on the Totnes to Paignton route. It is pictured here in 1917 with its wartime 'gasbag', used for fuel, upon its roof.

H. Pitts collection

2-6-2T No 4567 with the Plymouth Railway Circle 'farewell trip' on the Branch at Ashburton Station on 8th September 1962. Those posing in front of the train are, unfortunately, unrecorded apart from the late A. H. W. Christison, Dist Motive Power Supt, BR(WR), second from left.

The Sunday School Outing on 24th June 1959 has already drawn to a close as 2–6–2Ts Nos 4561 & 5573 return from Buckfastleigh to Totnes with the empty stock. This picture may, in fact, be a rare one of the only occasion in BR service when a 4575 class engine ran over this line as officially these engines, with the large capacity side tanks, were prohibited from using the Ashburton Branch (See text on page 75).

Peter W. Gray

2–6–2Ts Nos 4555 & 4561 pictured shortly after returning to Buckfastleigh from Teignmouth at the end of the Sunday School Outing on 29th June, 1960 (See text on page 75).

ENGINEERING AND OPERATING DATA

Pages 123 to 127 are reproduced from the Appendix to No 6 Section of the Service Time Tables, G.W.R. – April 1939; Alterations and Additions to the Appendix to No 6 Section of the Service Time Tables, Supplements No 6, 7 & 8, G.W.R. Instructions, Plymouth Division; No's 2431 dated February 1943, 2470 dated February 1944, and 2513 dated June 1945.

Pages 131 to 136 are reproduced from the Sectional Appendix to the Working Time Tables and Books of Rules and Regulations, B.R. (W.R.) Plymouth Traffic District, June 1960.

Pages 137 to 139 are Signal Box Diagrams of stations/junctions applicable to both branches. They were specially prepared for this book by members of the Historical Signalling Society.

Page 77 carries photographs of luggage labels for Totnes and Ashburton, others appertaining to the Ashburton branch appear on pages 68, 81, 99 & 139.

Photographs of tickets used on the branch appear on pages 40, 68, 80, 99, 134, 139 & 143.

ASHBURTON BRANCH

ASHBURTON

LEVEL
1 IN 60
LEVEL
$\frac{1}{60}$
$\frac{1}{80}$
LEVEL
$\frac{1}{137}$
$\frac{1}{62}$
$\frac{1}{92}$
LEVEL
1 IN 101
LEVEL

BUCKFASTLEIGH

1 IN 50
LEVEL
1 IN 110
LEVEL
1 IN 179
LEVEL
$\frac{1}{118}$
1 IN 293
1 IN 132
$\frac{1}{349}$
$\frac{1}{680}$
$\frac{1}{264}$
LEVEL
$\frac{1}{203}$

STAVERTON

1 IN 536
LEVEL
$\frac{1}{587}$
LEVEL
$\frac{1}{1815}$
$\frac{1}{550}$
LEVEL

JUNCTION WITH S.D.R.

0 1 2 3 4 5 6 7 8 9

TOTNES.

Down Goods Running Loop.

1. The Loop is 1,312 feet long, and is worked in accordance with the Standard Instructions in the General Appendix with the following modifications and additions :

2. The Facing and Trailing points of the Loop are worked from the Totnes Signal Box. A Catch Point is provided at each end, the one at London end being a spring point (not worked from the Box).

3. (a) The Loop must not be used as a Running line for trains conveying passengers, except when the usual Running line is not available, either by reason of accident or because it is occupied by the Engineers by previous arrangement with the District Traffic Manager.

(b) Whenever the Goods Running Loop is used for trains conveying passengers as set out above, Absolute Block Working must be maintained, and, in addition, all Facing and Catch points must be clipped and padlocked, the keys being kept by the Officer in charge of the operations. A loose lever for the Catch Point at London end of Loop is kept in the Totnes Signal Box.

4. **As soon as a train has passed on to the Loop and inside the points, it must be brought to a stand with the brake van as near as possible to the telephone box to enable the Guard (or Fireman in the case of a light engine) to promptly telephone to the Totnes Signalman an assurance that the train, with tail lamp attached, has arrived in clear of the Loop points.**

5. Down Freight Trains proceeding to the Loop may run direct into the Loop and pick up brakes there, except during fog or falling snow, when Brakes must be picked up at the Home Signal.

6. No wagons must be shunted off and allowed to stand in the Loop, except in case of emergency, when steps must be taken to clear them at the first opportunity.

7. The speed of trains passing over the Loop line must never exceed five miles per hour.

8. If it is necessary to back a train or engine into the Loop, this may be done, provided there is no train travelling in the Loop in the right direction towards it.

When a train has been backed into the Loop for the purpose of clearing the Main line, the Driver must give three short sharp whistles as soon as the train is placed clear of the Throw-off point, and the Guard or Shunter must telephone immediately to the Totnes Signalman informing him that the train is in clear of the Main line.

9. The special attention of Guards and Drivers is directed to Rule 147, it being important that the necessary assurance that train has arrived with tail lamp complete, in the Loop, clear of the Catch point, should be promptly telephoned to the Signalman in all cases.

Instructions for Working the Quay Line.

1. A Stop Board is fixed on the Quay line, 350 yards from the Catch point protecting the Main line.

2. The Shunter will be responsible for seeing that the points of the Loop on the Quay line are, after completion of work at the Loop, set normally for the Quay line.

3. Not more than one train must be permitted to be on the Quay line at the same time.

4. Trains must, as far as practicable, be drawn out from the Quay line, but when it is necessary to propel a train it must not exceed 15 wagons, and the Shunter must, when the wagons are propelled, walk alongside the leading wagon and signal to the Driver to ensure the train stopping well clear of the Quay line Signal when that Signal is at danger.

5. The maximum load of trains for the Quay is 35 wagons.

6. An engine with wagons attached may be run from Totnes to the Quay line, and vice versa, without a brake van in the rear, but a tail lamp must be carried on the last vehicle, and the Shunter must ride in or on the last wagon or walk alongside it.

7. Under no circumstances must any engine go further than the Stop Board, situated about three chains from the Main line side of the level crossing near the Main Road leading to Paignton.

Notice to Enginemen.

8. Trains proceeding to the Quay must stop at the Stop Board referred to in Clause 1, from which point they will be taken charge of by the Shunter, and when leaving again for the Down Main line must not proceed beyond the Quay line Signal until instructed to do so by the Shunter. This instruction does not apply to trains placed on the Quay line for refuging purposes.

Signalling of Non-Stopping Trains through the Platform Lines.

The Platform lines must not be used as Running lines for non-stopping Passenger Trains, except when the Main lines are not available, either by reason of accident or failure, or because they are occupied by the Engineers, by previous authority from the District Traffic Manager, in which circumstances the Platform Home Signal must not be lowered until the train has been brought quite or nearly to a stand.

When a Passenger train not booked to stop at Totnes is required to call specially necessitating diversion to the Platform Line, the Home Signal for that line must not be lowered until the train has been brought quite or nearly to a stand.

Assisting Parcels, Perishable or Empty Coaching Stock Trains.—Totnes to Rattery.

Down Parcels, Perishable or Empty Coaching Stock Trains requiring assistance from Totnes to Rattery, may be assisted in rear from Totnes, the Bank engine to run **uncoupled** to Rattery, where it will cease to push, and the train will run forward without stopping. The Bank engine will come to a stand in advance of the crossover road at Rattery.

The trains to carry usual tail lamp.

Engine in the rear must carry a tail lamp.

These provisions supplement, but do not cancel, those set out on Page 144 of the General Appendix.

Shunting.

1. When shunting in the Yard after dark, a tail lamp must, in all cases, be fixed on the last vehicle.

2. When it is necessary for shunting to take place between the Down Main line and the Sidings at Totnes, the men engaged in the shunting must perform the necessary coupling and uncoupling from the space between the Down Main line and the Station Sidings, **and must not stand between the two running lines.**

3. The Signals for controlling shunting operations will be given in accordance with Rule 117.

4. "Limit of Shunt" Board.—A "Limit of Shunt" Board is provided on the Up side for the Up Main line, 170 yards to the rear of the Up Main to Platform line facing points, and no shunting operations over the Up Main facing points must proceed beyond this Board.

ASHBURTON BRANCH.
Working of Passenger Trains.

The Passenger services on this Branch are worked without Guards, and the following instructions apply :—

1. The auto, or ordinary train, when consisting of not more than three coaches, or equivalent thereto, will be worked without a Guard. In the event of the train conveying more than three coaches, a Guard must be provided.

2. The station staff will be responsible for seeing that all doors are properly closed and fastened before the train leaves.

3. Auto, or ordinary trains, working on this Branch without Guards, must not convey more than three four-wheeled vehicles, as tail traffic and such vehicles must, in all cases, be vacuum fitted and connected. In no case must a train worked without a Guard exceed three eight-wheeled coaches, or two coaches and two four-wheeled vehicles, or one coach and three four-wheeled vehicles. The Station Master, or person in charge, must see that such vehicles are properly attached or detached by the Shunter or Porter, and that the tail lamp is transferred to proper position in each case.

4. All luggage, mails, parcels, etc., must be locked in the luggage bodies inaccessible to passengers, and the person in charge at each station will be responsible for seeing that the luggage body doors are properly closed and locked before the train leaves each station.

5. In the event of the engine becoming disabled in the Section and the application of Train Staff and Ticket Regulation 18 becoming necessary, the Fireman, before proceeding to the Staff Station for assistance, must protect the train in the opposite direction by putting down three detonators, 10 yards apart, at least 300 yards from the engine.

6. Special attention is directed to the instructions on page 132 of the General Appendix re "Working Auto Trains on Branch Lines without a Guard," and these instructions also apply in the event of a train being worked by an engine and three ordinary coaches, or equivalent thereto.

STAVERTON.
Level Crossing.

Except in respect of the heavier kinds of vehicular traffic referred to in the Standard Block Telegraph Regulations applicable to single lines, the level crossing gates must be kept across the line until trains are nearing the Home Signal.

Freight trains must not foul the level crossing by commencing shunting work until the road traffic which may be waiting has been allowed to pass.

Down Freight trains having station truck work to do at the platform must be drawn well clear of the crossing and the gates then placed across the line. The Guard must screw his van brake tightly on to prevent any backward movement.

The station trucks on Down trains must be formed next the rear van, and on Up trains next the engine.

Shunting operations must be stopped at the end of five minutes and the gates opened to the road, **unless it can be actually seen that no one is waiting to cross.**

BUCKFASTLEIGH.
Vehicles detached from Passenger Trains.

No vehicle detached from a Passenger train must be allowed to stand on the Main line.

ASHBURTON.
Hand Points, Crossover Road.

The normal position of the hand points of the crossover road at Ashburton, is for the Main line, and when the points are not actually in use, they must be kept padlocked in their normal position, and the key of the padlocks retained in the Booking Office.

Before the Starting Signal is lowered for a train to leave the Platform line, the person in charge is responsible for satisfying himself by personal observation that the points of the crossover road are properly set and padlocked in their normal position, and similar precautions must be observed by the person in charge before the Down Home Signal is lowered to admit a Down train.

At night the points must be so set and locked (after all vehicles are back over them), that in case such vehicles should break loose, or be blown out, they would run into the Engine Shed line, and so prevent their going over the incline at lower end of Yard.

Engine running round Train.

The Guard, or Signalman when no Guard on train, will be responsible for the braking back of the trains to allow the engine to run around. This is important, as an incline of 1 in 60 exists at the Totnes end of the Yard.

COUPLING AND UNCOUPLING OF ENGINES OF PASSENGER TRAINS EXCEPT WHERE OTHERWISE SHOWN.

The following arrangements will apply to the coupling and uncoupling of engines in the Plymouth Division.

Station.	Work performed by Fireman.	Work performed by Traffic Department.
Ashburton	Departure	Arrival and Shunting.
Totnes	Main Line and Branch Departure	Arrival and Shunting.

STATIONS AT WHICH LOOSE SCREW COUPLINGS ARE KEPT—PLYMOUTH DIVISION.

Referring to page 145 of the General Appendix, Emergency Loose Screw Couplings are provided at the following Stations :—

Station.	Number of Couplings. Type.		
	4	5	6
Ashburton	—	1	—
Buckfastleigh	—	1	—
Totnes	—	2	2

FROM	TO	Description of Staff, etc.		Where Electric Train Token or Train Staff and Tickets are kept.	Persons at Station or Junction responsible for exchanging Token or Ticket when on duty.	Person responsible when aforesaid man is not on duty.	REMARKS.
		Colour.	Shape.				
Totnes ...	Buckfastleigh ...	Red	Square	Signal Box, Totnes ...	Signalman† ...	...	Train Staff and Ticket.
Buckfastleigh ...	Ashburton ...	Blue	Round	Booking Office, Buckfastleigh ...	Signalman ...	...	Train Staff and Ticket. See page 51.
Totnes ...	Totnes Quay	—	—	Booking Office, Ashburton ...	" —	—	

Inclines steeper than 1 in 200—continued.

Ashburton Branch.

Incline situated between	Length of Incline.	Gradient one foot in	Falling towards	Places at which Notice Boards have been fixed and at which trains must stop to put down brakes.	Modifications of or additions to the Standard Instructions for working Inclines.
BRANCHES.					
Ashburton and Buckfastleigh	2 m.	Max. 60 with varying lengths of lesser gradients	Buckfastleigh ...		
Buckfastleigh and Staverton	3¾ m.	Max. 50 with varying lengths of lesser gradients	Staverton ...		

40

Stations in the Plymouth Division where Engines can take Water—continued.

Branches.

Station.	Where Cranes, etc., are situated.
Ashburton ...	Locomotive Engine Shed.

STATIONS IN THE PLYMOUTH DIVISION WHERE ENGINES CAN TAKE WATER.

Add :

Station.	Where cranes, etc., are situated.
Totnes	East end Up Goods Loop.
Wearde	West end of Down Goods Running Loop.
Lostwithiel	East end Up Goods Loop.

Page 51.
Insert :

TOTNES.
Up Goods Loop.

1. The loop is level. It is 1,426 feet in length and will accommodate two engines, 60 wagons and van and is worked in accordance with the Regulations for signalling trains and engines by Permissive Block System over Goods Running Loop Lines and other Permissive Lines, as shewn on pages 86-88 of the Book of Regulations for Train Signalling on Double and Single Lines and extracts therefrom shewn on pages 57 and 58 of the General Appendix to the Rule Book, so far as they apply.

2. The Facing and Trailing Points of the loop, also the catch points at both ends, are worked from Totnes Signal Box. The catch points and trailing points at the "Paddington" end are operated by motor.

3. No loose wagons must be detached and allowed to stand in the loop except in case of emergency, when steps must be taken to clear them at the first opportunity. After sunset or during fog or falling snow, a red light must be exhibited on the rear and a white light on the front of such vehicle or vehicles.

4. The speed of trains when leaving the loop must not exceed 10 m.p.h.

5. Assistant engines may be allowed to come to the rear of Up Freight trains standing in the loop and assist the train to Dainton. Owing to the reverse curves at the junction with the main line at the East end of the loop Assistant engines must not push until clear of this connection.

Page 51.

TOTNES.
INSTRUCTIONS FOR WORKING THE QUAY LINE.

Amend : Instructions to be amended as follows :

1. A Stop Board is fixed on the Quay Line 350 yards from the catchpoint protecting the main line and gates are provided at the Racecourse Level Crossing. The normal position of the gates is across the line and the key of the padlock securing the gates must be kept in Totnes signal box.

2. The Shunter is responsible for the safe working of trains over the level crossing and, before proceeding to the Quay Line, must obtain the key of the gates from the Signalman. All trains proceeding to Parklands, Racecourse, or the Bacon Factory sidings must come to a stand at the Stop Board, from which point the Shunter will take charge of them. They must be again brought to a stand at the Racecourse Level Crossing for the Shunter to open the crossing gates and secure them across the roadways. After the train has passed over the level crossing the Shunter must replace and secure the gates in the normal position.

3. Before permitting any shunting movements to be made which will foul the level crossing the Shunter must open the crossing gates and secure them across the roadway.

4. After completion of work at Parklands, Racecourse or Bacon Factory Sidings, the Shunter must set all points normally for the Quay Line and the train must be brought to a stand on each side of Racecourse Level Crossing to enable the gates to be dealt with as shewn in Clause 2 and the Shunter to rejoin the train. The key of the gates must be returned to the Signalman on arrival at Totnes Station.

5 Not more than one train must be permitted on the Quay Line at one time except that, if necessary, in connection with traffic from the Racecourse Sidings, an additional engine may proceed on to the Quay Line after a clear understanding has been arrived at by all concerned. The Driver of this engine must bring it to a stand at the Stop Board from which point he must work under the instructions of the Shunter.

6. Trains must. as far as practicable, be drawn on to or out from the Quay Line, but when it is necessary to propel a train, it must not exceed 15 wagons, and the Shunter must, when the wagons are propelled, walk alongside the leading wagon and signal to the Driver to ensure the train stopping well clear of the crossing gates or the Quay Line signal when that signal is at danger. When trains are drawn on to or out from the Quay Line, Drivers must not proceed beyond the Stop Board or the Quay Line signal until instructed to do so by the Shunter.

7. The maximum load of trains to and from the sidings on the Quay Line is 35 wagons.

8. An engine, with wagons attached, may be run from Totnes to the Quay Line, and vice versa, without a Brake Van in the rear, but a tail lamp must be carried on the last vehicle, and the Shunter must ride in or on the last wagon or walk alongside it.

9. An engine Stop Board is fixed 44 yards from the Totnes-Paignton main road level crossing and no engines must proceed beyond this board.

10. The Quay Line may be used as a refuge siding for Up main line freight trains or light engines, provided there is no other train or engine working on the Quay Line. Any freight train placed on the Quay Line for refuging purposes must not exceed engine, 60 wagons and van, and when the train is being set back on to the Quay Line the Guard must keep a good lookout and be prepared to apply the hand brake to ensure the train does not foul the Racecourse level crossing.

Name of Crossing.	Where Situated.		Whether Block Post.	If not a Block Post whether Gatekeeper Indicators, or Bells are provided.	Whether there are signals.	Whether the Gates are interlocked with the Signals.
	Between	And				
Ashburton Branch Staverton .. Staverton Station ..	Totnes .. At Staverton Station	Staverton	No Yes	Gatekeeper —	No Yes	No, Yes
Totnes Quay Line. Race Marsh ..	Totnes ..	Totnes Quay ..	No.	—	No.	No.

Page 36.

REFUGE SIDINGS AND RUNNING LOOPS.

Amend existing and insert new entries as shewn below :

Station	Up or Down		Number of Wagons Siding holds in addition to large Engine and Van		When closed and not available for use
	Down	Up	Down	Up	
Totnes Loops ..	1	1	56	60b	See Special instructions for working, page 51. **b**—Will hold two engines, van and 60 wagons.

STATIONS IN PLYMOUTH DIVISION WHERE RE-RAILING RAMPS ARE KEPT.

Station.	Where stored.
Ashburton	Goods Shed.
Totnes	Stores, east end Down Platform.

INSTRUCTIONS IN CONNECTION WITH THE WORKING OF THE ROYAL TRAIN.

JOURNEY—PADDINGTON TO TOTNES, TUESDAY, OCTOBER 28th AND WEDNESDAY, OCTOBER 29th, 1947.

OPENING OF SIGNAL BOXES—The following Signal Boxes to be open specially:

Calcot	To remain open until the Royal Train has cleared.
Grafton East Junction	To remain open until the Royal Train has cleared.
Woodlands	To remain open until the Royal Train has cleared.
Keinton Mandeville	To open at 9.30 p.m. and remain open until the Train has cleared.
Charlton Mackrell	To open at 9.30 p.m.
Long Sutton & Pitney	To open at 9.30 p.m. and remain open until the Train has cleared.
Poole Siding	To open at 10.0 p.m. and remain open until the Train has cleared.
Silverton	To open at 10.30 p.m. and remain open until the Train has cleared.
Stoke Canon Junction	To remain open until the Train has cleared.
St. Thomas	To remain open until the Train has cleared.
Parson's Tunnel	To open at 10.30 p.m. and remain open until the Train has cleared.
Teignmouth Old Quay	To open at 11.0 p.m and remain open until the Train has cleared.
Bishopsteignton	To remain open until the Train has cleared.
Staverton	Continuously from 7.30 a.m. October 28th to 7.30 p.m. October 30th.
Buckfastleigh	Continuously from 7.30 a.m. October 28th to 7.30 p.m. October 30th.

TUNNELS.—(See Clause 16, General Instructions, page 35.)

Somerton	Between Castle Cary and Athelney. Length 1,053 yards.
Whiteball	Between Wellington and Burlescombe. Length 1,092 yards.
Kennaway	Between Dawlish and Teignmouth. Length 209 yards.
Coryton	Between Dawlish and Teignmouth. Length 231 yards.
Phillot	Between Dawlish and Teignmouth. Length 55 yards.
Clerk's	Between Dawlish and Teignmouth. Length 66 yards.
Parson's	Between Dawlish and Teignmouth. Length 512 yards.
Dainton	Between Aller Junction and Totnes. Length 264 yards.

TOTNES

1. The Station Master will be personally responsible for seeing the platforms and footbridge are clear of all unauthorised persons and the waiting-rooms closed, and the doors locked, 15 minutes before the Royal Train is due to arrive, until it has passed on to the Ashburton Branch.

2. Engine No. 5094 to draw the Royal Train from Totnes on to the Ashburton Branch must be placed in the Up Goods Loop 30 minutes before the Royal Train is due to arrive and stand just inside catch-points No. 64. Except for this engine, the Up Goods Loop must be unoccupied for 30 minutes before the Royal Train arrives and so remain until the train has proceeded on to the Ashburton Branch.

3. No train, or engine, must be allowed to stand on the Up main line, or in the Up and Down Platform lines, 30 minutes prior to the arrival of the Royal Train, and until after it has proceeded on to the Branch, and Points Nos. 63 and 65 are in their normal position, and Points No. 63 clipped and padlocked in that position. No engine, or train, must be allowed to stand on the Totnes Quay Line 30 minutes before the Royal Train is due to pass, and until the train has proceeded on to the Ashburton Branch.

4. The Signalman at Totnes must send the "Blocking Back outside Home Signal" to, and receive acknowledgment from Tigley 10 minutes before the Royal Train is due to arrive. The "Obstruction Removed" signal may be sent when the Train has proceeded in clear on to the Ashburton Branch and the Up Loop Facing Points No. 63 have been re-set for the loop and clipped and padlocked.

5. The Totnes Down Main Distant Signal will be at "Caution." The Totnes Down Main Home, Down Main Intermediate Home, Down Main Inner Intermediate Home and Down Main Inner Home Signals must be lowered in that sequence immediately the Royal Train operates track circuits Nos. 110AT, 110T., 109T., and 108T. to the rear of these signals respectively. (This instruction modifies the provisions of Rule 39 (a).)

6. The Royal Train must arrive on the Down main line and must be brought to a stand with the centre of the footplate of the leading engine opposite the white light provided on a post on the Driver's side at 222 m. 71¼ c. The Guards must apply their hand-brakes.

7. The District Inspector must make arrangements for working by Pilotman to be introduced between Totnes and Buckfastleigh after the 6.45 p.m. ex Totnes has cleared the section, in readiness for the Royal Train to be worked to the stabling point on the Ashburton Branch. The Assistant District Inspector must be appointed Pilotman, and he must take and retain possession of the Train Staff, and accompany every movement to and from the Branch.

8. After the Train has come to a stand the Signalman must reverse Points Nos. 65, 64, and the crossover road No. 57, and after the District Inspector has satisfied himself that the road is properly set, and Catch-points No. 64 and crossover Points No. 57 clipped and padlocked, he must arrange for Engine No. 5094, which will be standing in the Up Goods Loop, to be brought out on to the Down main line to the rear of the Train, the Pilotman accompanying the engine. A Handsignalman will be provided at crossover Points No. 57. As soon as the engine has passed on to the Down main line the District Inspector must arrange for Points No. 64 to be unclipped and restored to their normal position. Points No. 63 must then be set for the Ashburton Branch. The Fireman of Engine No. 5094 must couple the engine to the Royal Train, after which the train engines must be detached by the Fireman of Engine No. 5055.

9. The Signalman at Totnes must ask "Is Line Clear?" from Staverton for the Royal Train as soon as the engine to take the Train on to the Branch has arrived on the Down Main. The Signalman at Staverton, before returning "Line Clear" to Totnes, must send the "Blocking Back" signal to, and receive acknowledgment from, Buckfastleigh.

10. The Totnes Station Master must personally satisfy himself that the engine for working the train to the Ashburton Branch has been attached, and the train engines have been detached, and the tail-lamps are in the correct positions on the Train. After the Superintendent of the Line's Inspector has assured the Station Master that all is in order for the Train to proceed, the Station Master must give the "right away" signal to the rear Guard.

11. The Royal Train must come to a stand on the Ashburton Branch with the centre of the footplate of the engine opposite the white light on a post which will be provided on the Driver's side, at 1m. 14½c., and the hand brakes must be fully applied. The engine must remain attached to the train until it leaves for St. Austell.

12. After the train has passed in clear on to the Ashburton Branch, the District Inspector must arrange for the Up Loop Facing Points No. 63 to be clipped and padlocked in their normal position and hand the key to the Superintendent of the Line's Inspector.

BUCKFASTLEIGH

1. The Station Master, after departure of the 6.45 p.m. ex Totnes, must arrange for Points No. 10 to be reversed, clipped and padlocked, and personally take the key by taxi to the Station Master at Totnes, and the latter must hand this key to the Superintendent of the Line's Inspector on arrival of the Royal Train.

2. The Pilotman must obtain the key from the Superintendent of the Line's Inspector and hand it to the Station Master at Totnes on arrival on the day of the journey from Totnes to St. Austell. The Buckfastleigh Station Master must proceed to Totnes by taxi and obtain the key of the padlock of points No. 10 from the Station Master.

TIME TABLE OF ROYAL TRAIN—DEVONPORT TO TOTNES—*continued.*

WEDNESDAY, OCTOBER 29th—*continued.*

Distances from Devonport		PRINCIPAL STATIONS AND INTERMEDIATE SIGNAL BOXES.	TIMES.	REMARKS.
Miles	Ch'ns		P.M.	
4	5	Tavistock Junction .. pass	6.14	Speed not to exceed 35 miles per hour at Tavistock Junction between 243 miles 18 chains and 243 miles 5 chains.
7	75	Hemerdon .. .. ,,	6.25	
9	47	Cornwood	—	Speed not to exceed 50 miles per hour west and east of Cornwood between 237 miles 50 chains and 237 miles 10 chains.
12	2	Ivybridge .. .. .,	—	Speed not to exceed 50 miles per hour west and east of Ivybridge between 235 miles 20 chains and 234 miles 60 chains.
14	18	Bittaford Platform .. ,,	—	Speed not to exceed 50 miles per hour west and east of Bittaford between 233 miles 10 chains and 232 miles 70 chains.
15	33	Wrangaton Tunnel .. ,,	—	General Instructions (clause 16, page 85) in regard to the examination and protection of Tunnels must be observed.
17	41	Brent .. .. .. ,,	6.41	Speed not to exceed 50 miles per hour west and east of Brent between 230 miles 20 chains and 229 miles 50 chains.
18	73	Marley Tunnel (Up and Down)	—	General Instructions (clause 16, page 85) in regard to the examination and protection of Tunnels must be observed. The 9.10 a.m. Manchester to Plymouth to be terminated at Newton Abbot.
19	66	Rattery .. .. .. ,,	—	Speed not to exceed 50 miles per hour west of Totnes between 227 miles 30 chains and 223 mile post. The 1.30 p.m. Paddington to Penzance to call at Totnes and Brent and be held at Rattery until the Royal Train has passed. The 6.15 p.m. Plymouth to Bristol to be held at Rattery until the Royal Train has cleared Ashburton Junction.
24	30	Totnes .. .. { arr. { dep.	6.53 7. 5	The 6.45 p.m. Totnes to Ashburton to be suspended. For detailed instructions for dealing with the Royal Train at Totnes, see pages 19 and 20. Saloons Nos. 76 and 77 to be fully charged with gas, and watered to capacity at Totnes Station. Detach Engines Nos. 5069 and 7818. Attach Engine No. 5094.
24	49	Ashburton Junction .. pass	7. 6	Speed not to exceed 10 miles per hour when passing from Main Line to Branch Line, and up to the Stabling Point on the Ashburton Branch.
25	41	**TOTNES** .. .. .. **arr.** **(Stabling Point on Ashburton Branch.)** **(Between 1 mile and 1¼ mile posts.)**	7.15	

TIME TABLE OF ROYAL TRAIN—TOTNES TO KINGSWEAR, THURSDAY, OCTOBER 30th.

FORMATION (*FROM ENGINE*) **OF ROYAL TRAIN LEAVING TOTNES** (*STABLING POINT*) **AND ARRIVING KINGSWEAR :—**

	BRAKE FIRST .. .. No. 5154	
	SLEEPING SALOON .. .. „ 477	
	DINING SALOON .. .. „ 77	
	SALOON .. .. „ 806	
L.M. & S.	SLEEPING SALOON .. .. „ 495	
Co.'s	SALOON .. .. „ 807	480 tons.
Stock	DINING SALOON .. .. „ 76	
	SALOON .. .. „ 798	
	SALOON .. .. „ 799	
	SALOON .. .. „ 805	
	BRAKE FIRST .. .. „ 5155	

Length of Train (excluding Engines) .. .. 724 feet 10 inches.

The Train will carry TWO G.W. standard pattern white-painted Tail Lamps. (Important—see paragraph 2, page 34.)

The engine Headlamps and the Tail lamps must be lighted before leaving Totnes (Stabling Point), and the Headlamps of the Engines working the Train from Totnes to Aller Junction, and from Aller Junction to Kingswear, also the Tail Lamps, must be lighted before departure from each point.

The Train will run on the Main Line throughout the journey; Up Main Line at Aller Junction, thence to the Kingswear Branch Down Main Line.

NOTE :—The Train reverses at Totnes Station and Aller Junction.

ADVICE OF DEPARTURE TIME OF TRAIN FROM TOTNES.

Station Master, Totnes, to advise **District Traffic Manager,** Plymouth, **Divisional Superintendent,** Exeter, and **Station Master,** Kingswear, the time the Train leaves Totnes.

· THE PERMANENT AND TEMPORARY SPEED RESTRICTIONS MUST BE STRICTLY OBSERVED.

Distances from Totnes		PRINCIPAL STATIONS AND INTERMEDIATE SIGNAL BOXES.	TIMES.	REMARKS.
Miles	Ch'ns		A.M.	
—	—	**TOTNES** .. .. .. dep. (**Stabling Point on Ashburton Branch**).	8.40	For detailed instructions for dealing with the Royal Train at Totnes, see page 20. Engine No. 5058 forward. **Speed not to exceed 10 miles per hour from the Stabling Point to the Up Main Line at Ashburton Junction.**
—	72	Ashburton Junction .. pass	8.49	
1	11	Totnes .. .. { arr (Up Main Line). { dep.	8.50 9. 0	Detach Engine No. 5058. Attach Engines Nos. 5069 and 5055. The 7.32 a.m. Plymouth to Newton Abbot to be terminated at Brent. The 8.35 a.m. Newton Abbot to Plymouth to start from Brent. The 8.30 a.m. Plymouth to Paddington to call additionally at Brent and Totnes and be held at Dainton Box until the Royal Train has cleared Aller Junction. The 8.45 a.m. Plymouth to Crewe to be held at Totnes until the Royal Train has cleared Aller Junction.
1	30	Ashburton Junction .. pass	9. 1	**Speed not to exceed 40 miles per hour on Dainton Incline between 222 mile post and 218 miles 20 chains.**

TOTNES TO ASHBURTON (ASHBURTON BRANCH)

STAVERTON.

STATION LEVEL CROSSING.

Except in respect of the heavier kinds of vehicular traffic referred to in the Standard Regulations, the level crossing gates must be kept across the line until trains are nearing the station.

Freight trains must not foul the level crossing by commencing shunting work until the road traffic which may be waiting has been allowed to pass.

Shunting operations must be stopped at the end of five minutes and the gates opened to the road, unless it can be actually seen that no one is waiting to cross.

BUCKFASTLEIGH.

BLASTING AT MESSRS. HOARE BROS. LTD.'s QUARRY, PRIDHAMSLEIGH, BUCKFASTLEIGH.

This Quarry is situated on the Up Side of the line between Ashburton and Buckfastleigh at 7m. 38ch. and blasting is undertaken each weekday. In order to ensure the safety of rail traffic the following instructions must be observed:—

1.   Permission for blasting must not be given if there is a train or engine on the Ashburton side of Buckfastleigh Station.

2.   Blasting will take place between the hours of 9.45 a.m. and 10.15 a.m. each weekday.

3.   At 9.35 a.m. each weekday, the Ganger will present himself at Buckfastleigh Station and if it is permissible for blasting to proceed, the Station Master or person in charge will advise the Ganger accordingly.

4.   If permission for blasting is given, the Ganger must place three detonators on the rail at Buckfastleigh and exhibit a red flag in such a position as to prevent any train proceeding in the direction of Ashburton. The Ganger will then notify the Firm's Foreman that blasting may take place. On receiving an assurance from the Firm's Foreman that blasting has been completed, and satisfying himself the line is safe for rail traffic, the Ganger must return to Buckfastleigh Station, advise the Station Master or person in charge accordingly and withdraw the detonators and red flag.

5.   If a second, or alternative, period for blasting is required this will be between 11.50 a.m. and 12.15 p.m., but the Firm's Foreman at the Quarry must first obtain the agreement of the Station Master at Buckfastleigh, who will establish contact with the Ganger for the length concerned so that the protective measures detailed in Clause 4 may be undertaken.

6.   No departure from the times laid down must be made without a clear understanding being reached between the Firm's Foreman at the Quarry and the Station Master or person in charge at Buckfastleigh.

7.   In the event of alternative times being agreed, the procedure previously outlined to ensure the safe working of the line must be adopted.

ASHBURTON.

ENGINE RUNNING ROUND TRAIN.

The Guard will be responsible for the braking back of the train to allow the engine to run around. This is important as an incline of 1 in 60 exists at the Totnes end of the Yard.

USE OF TOW ROPES.

Owing to the formation of the Sidings at Ashburton the use of tow ropes in connection with shunting operations is specially authorised.

LOADING OF GRAIN HOPPERS ON SINGLE LINE.

Messrs. E. Tucker & Sons Ltd. rent the ex Locomotive Shed as a grain drying store and load direct from this store into grain hoppers standing on the Single Line. In connection with this arrangement, the following special instructions must be observed by trainmen:

Down Freight trains must stop dead at the Stop Board provided on the post of the disused Down Home Signal and must not proceed beyond that point until after the arrival of the Ashburton Checker who will, provided he is certain no loading work by Messrs. Tucker's employees is in progress, pilot the train into Ashburton Station.

One Engine in Steam Working

BRANCHES

TOTNES TO ASHBURTON

Description of Block Signalling on Principal Running line. Dots indicate Block Posts	Stations, Signal Boxes, etc.	Distance from Signal Box next above		Running lines			Loops and Refuge Sidings			Runaway Catch Points—Spring or unworked Trailing Points		Engine Whistles s—short L—long				C—crow
												DOWN		UP		
		M.	Yds.	Additional UP	Principal	Additional DOWN	Description	Standage Wagons E. & V.	Line	Position	Gradient (Rising unless otherwise shown) 1 in.	Main	Relief or Goods	Main	Relief or Goods	Remarks
	Totnes															
	Staverton	3	506													
	Buckfastleigh	3	1254													
	Ashburton	2	792													

TABLE D. 2.

LINES WORKED UNDER THE ELECTRIC TOKEN, TRAIN STAFF AND TICKET OR ONE ENGINE IN STEAM ARRANGEMENTS

(Handling of Token or Staff).

The following is a list of places where persons other than Signalmen are authorised to receive or deliver the Token or Staff:—

Section of Line.	Token or Staff Station.	Person authorised to receive or deliver Token or Staff.
TOTNES TO ASHBURTON.		
Totnes to Ashburton	Totnes	Porter.

TABLE F.

PROPELLING TRAINS OR VEHICLES.

When trains or vehicles are being propelled in accordance with Rule 149 the undermentioned conditions must be complied with. The sections of line where propelling outside station limits is authorised are shown below.

When vehicles are propelled or gravitated within station limits on a running line or loop, the Guard, Shunter, or person in charge must, except in the case of the movement of freight vehicles in charge of a Guard or Shunter, ride in the leading or first suitable vehicle.

When propelling freight vehicles outside station limits a Guard's brake van must be the leading vehicle, unless otherwise indicated, and the Guard or Shunter must ride therein.

In the case of coaching stock vehicles or where authority is given to propel freight vehicle without a brake van leading the Guard or Shunter must ride in the leading suitable vehicle.

Drivers will not be relieved of responsibility for observing fixed signals, but the Guard, Shunter, or person in charge must keep a sharp lookout, warn any person who may be on or near the line, observe fixed signals and be prepared to give any necessary hand signal to the Driver. Drivers must keep a sharp look out and be prepared to act immediately upon any signal which may be given by the Guard, Shunter, or person in charge.

The speed must not exceed 20 m.p.h., and down inclines steeper than 1 in 200, through station platforms and over level crossings must not exceed 15 m.p.h. (This paragraph does not apply to Officers' Specials).

The engine whistle must be sounded when approaching stations and level crossings, also where there is not a good view of the line ahead.

Where the line is on a failing gradient a sufficient number of wagon brakes must be pinned down whenever there is a doubt as to whether the brake van will hold the train should it become divided, or where there is no brake van attached.

In all cases where coaching stock or fitted vehicles are authorised to be propelled, the automatic brake must be connected up and in use.

Vehicles conveying passengers must not be propelled under this arrangement except in the case of items marked " P " :—

From.	To.	Line.	Number of vehicles and Special conditions.
Totnes	Totnes Quay ..	Single	Not more than 15 wagons may be propelled. Shunter must walk alongside leading vehicle. Instructions shown on page 75
Totnes Quay ..	Totnes	Single	Not more than 15 wagons may be propelled. Shunter must walk alongside leading vehicle. Instructions shown on page 75

TABLE J. 1—*continued.*

Incline situated between. **TOTNES TO ASHBURTON.**	Length of Incline.	Ruling Gradient— One in.	Falling towards.	Modifications of, or additions to, the General Instructions for Working Inclines.
Ashburton and Buckfastleigh ..	2 m.	Maximum 60 with varying lengths of lesser gradients	Buckfastleigh	
Buckfastleigh and Staverton ..	3¾ m.	Maximum 50 with varying lengths of lesser gradients	Staverton	

133

TABLE H 1.

WORKING OF FREIGHT VEHICLES WITHOUT A BRAKE VAN IN REAR.

Set out below is a list of places where Freight vehicles (in accordance with Rule 153(*b*)) may be worked without a brake van in rear.

One wagon of coal or stores for Signal Boxes and Stations, or the empty wagon in connection therewith, may be worked without a brake van between any two Signal Boxes, provided the Signal Boxes concerned are not more than one mile apart.

From.	To.	Line.	No. of vehicles and Special Conditions.
DAINTON (EXCL.)	**TO PENZANCE.**		
Totnes	Totnes Quay ..	Single ..	A Shunter must ride on or in the last wagon or walk alongside it. Instructions shown on page 75.
Totnes Quay ..	Totnes	Single ..	A Shunter must ride on or in the last wagon or walk alongside it. Instructions shown on page 75.

TABLE P.

LEVEL CROSSING GATES—OPENING AND CLOSING BY TRAINMEN.

The following is a list of level crossings where, in the absence of a Crossing Keeper, the gates must be opened and closed by the Trainmen.

Trains must be brought to a stand well clear of the gates, after which the gates must be unlocked and opened for the passage of the train over the crossing. Except as shown below the gates must be unlocked and opened by the Fireman of the train. When the train has passed over the crossing, the Guard, or Shunter where indicated (or Fireman in the case of a light engine) must close the gates across the railway and re-lock them, the Driver taking care not to proceed on his journey until he has received an "All Right" signal from the Guard. Enginemen and Guards concerned must see that they are supplied with keys of the gates.

Any defects in the gates or the locks securing them or in the lamps must be reported immediately by the Guard or Fireman to the Station Master concerned.

Name of Crossing.	Situated at or between.	Remarks.
TOTNES TO TOTNES QUAY.		
Racecourse ..	Totnes and Totnes Quay	Crossing gates to be opened and closed by Shunter accompanying the train.
TOTNES TO ASHBURTON.		
Staverton ...	Totnes and Staverton	

134

LOCAL INSTRUCTIONS.

TOTNES.

INSTRUCTIONS FOR WORKING THE QUAY LINE.

1.   A Stop Board is fixed on the Quay Line 350 yards from the catchpoint protecting the main line and gates are provided at the Level Crossing known as the Racecourse Level Crossing.   The normal position of the gates is across the line and the key of the padlock securing the gates must be kept in Totnes Signal box.

2.   The Shunter is responsible for the safe working of trains over the Level Crossing and before proceeding to the Quay Line must obtain the key of the gates from the Signalman.   All trains proceeding to Parklands, the Old Racecourse or the Bacon Factory Sidings must come to a stand at the Stop Board, from which point the Shunter will take charge of them.   They must be again brought to a stand at the Racecourse Level Crossing for the Shunter to open the crossing gates and secure them across the roadways.   After the train has passed over the Level Crossing the Shunter must replace and secure the gates in the normal position.

3.   Before permitting any shunting movements to be made which will foul the level crossing the Shunter must open the crossing gates and secure them across the roadway.

4.   After completion of work at Parklands, the Old Racecourse Sidings or Bacon Factory Sidings, the Shunter must set all points normally for the Quay Line and the train must be brought to a stand on each side of Racecourse Level Crossing to enable the gates to be dealt with as shown in clause 2 and the Shunter to rejoin the train.   The key of the gate must be returned to the Signalman on arrival at Totnes Station.

5.   Not more than one train must be permitted on the Quay Line at the same time.

6.   Trains must, as far as practicable, be drawn on to or out from the Quay Line, but when it is necessary to propel a train, it must not exceed 15 wagons, and the Shunter must, when the wagons are propelled, walk alongside the leading wagon and signal to the Driver to ensure the train stopping well clear of the crossing gates or the Quay Line signal when that signal is at danger.   When trains are drawn on to or out from the Quay Line, Drivers must not proceed beyond the Stop Board, or the Quay Line signal until instructed to do so by the Shunter.

7.   The maximum load of trains to and from the sidings on the Quay Line is 35 wagons.

8.   An engine, with wagons attached, may be run from Totnes to the Quay Line, and vice versa, without a Brake Van in the rear, but a tail lamp must be carried on the last vehicle, and the Shunter must ride in or on the last wagon or walk alongside it.

9.   An engine Stop Board is fixed 44 yards from the Totnes-Paignton main road level crossing and no engines must proceed beyond this board.

DOWN GOODS LOOP.

1.   The Loop is worked in accordance with the Regulations for Train Signalling by the Permissive Block System with the following modifications and additions:—

2.   As soon as a train has passed on to the Loop and inside the points it must be brought to a stand with the brake van as near as possible to the telephone to enable the Guard (or Fireman in the case of a light engine) to promptly telephone to the Totnes Signalman an assurance that the train with tail lamp attached has arrived in clear of the Loop points.

3.   Down Freight Trains proceeding to the Loop may run direct into the Loop and pick up brakes there, except during fog or falling snow when brakes must be picked up at the Home Signal.

4.   No wagons must be shunted off and allowed to stand in the Loop except in case of emergency, when steps must be taken to clear them at the first opportunity.   After sunset or during fog or falling snow a red light must be exhibited on the rear and a white light on the front of such vehicle or vehicles.

5.   The speed of trains passing over the Loop Line must never exceed five miles per hour.

6.　When a train has been backed into the Loop for the purpose of clearing the Main line, the Driver must give three short sharp whistles as soon as the train is placed clear of the catch point, and the Guard or Shunter must telephone immediately to the Totnes Signalman informing him that the train is in clear of the Main Line.

7.　The special attention of Guards and Drivers is directed to Rule 147 as it is important that the necessary assurance that the train has arrived with tail lamp complete, in the Loop, clear of the catch point, should be promptly telephoned to the Signalman in all cases.

UP GOODS LOOP.

1.　The Loop is worked in accordance with the Regulations for Train Signalling by the Permissive Block System with the following modifications and additions:—

2.　The trailing points and Catch Points at the London end of the Loop are worked by motor.

3.　No loose wagons must be detached and allowed to stand in the Loop except in case of emergency when steps must be taken to clear them at the first opportunity. After sunset or during fog or falling snow a red light must be exhibited on the rear and a white light on the front of such vehicle or vehicles.

4.　The speed of trains when leaving the Loop must not exceed ten miles per hour.

5.　Assistant engines may be allowed to come to the rear of Up Freight trains standing in the Up Loop and assist the train to Dainton. Owing to the reverse curves at the junction with the Main line at the East end of the Loop, Assistant engines must not push until clear of this connection.

SIGNALLING OF NON-STOPPING TRAINS THROUGH THE PLATFORM LINES.

The Platform Lines must not be used as Running lines for non-stopping Passenger trains except when the Main Lines are not available either by reason of accident or failure or because they are occupied by the Engineers, by previous authority from the District Traffic Superintendent, in which circumstances the Platform Home Signal must not be lowered until the Train has been brought quite or nearly to a stand.

When a Passenger train not booked to stop at Totnes is required to call specially necessitating diversion to the Platform Line the Home Signal for that line must not be lowered until the train has been brought quite or nearly to a stand.

SHUNTING.

When it is necessary for shunting to take place between the Down Main Line and the Sidings at Totnes, the men engaged in the shunting must perform the necessary coupling and uncoupling from the space between the Down Main Line and the Station Siding and must not stand between the two running lines.

" LIMIT OF SHUNT " INDICATOR.

A " Limit of Shunt " Board is provided on the Up Side for the Up Main line, 170 yards to the rear of the Up Main to Platform line facing points and no shunting operations over the Up Main facing points must proceed beyond this Board.

VEHICLES LEFT ON RUNNING LINE.

In any case where a vehicle is detached after dark, or during fog or falling snow at either the Up or Down Platform a red light must be placed on the front as well as on the rear of the vehicle until it is removed from the Main line.

Under no circumstances must loose vehicles be left on the Up or Down Through Roads.

TELEPHONE AT UP BRANCH HOME SIGNAL.

A telephone giving communication to the Totnes Signalman is provided at the Up Branch Home Signal to enable the provision of Rule 55 (*a*) to be carried out when a train is detained at the signal.

TOTNES

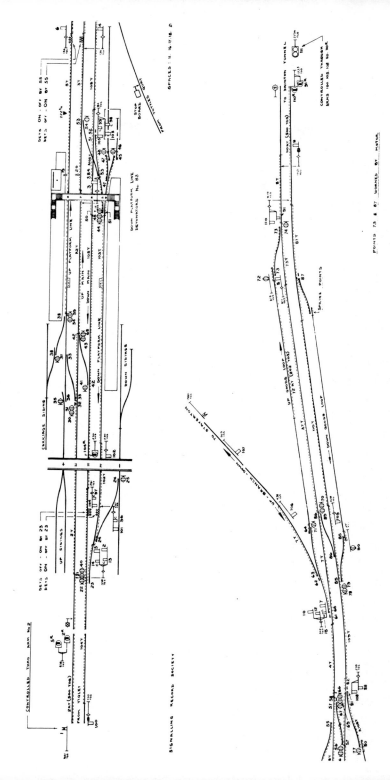

SIGNALLING RECORD SOCIETY

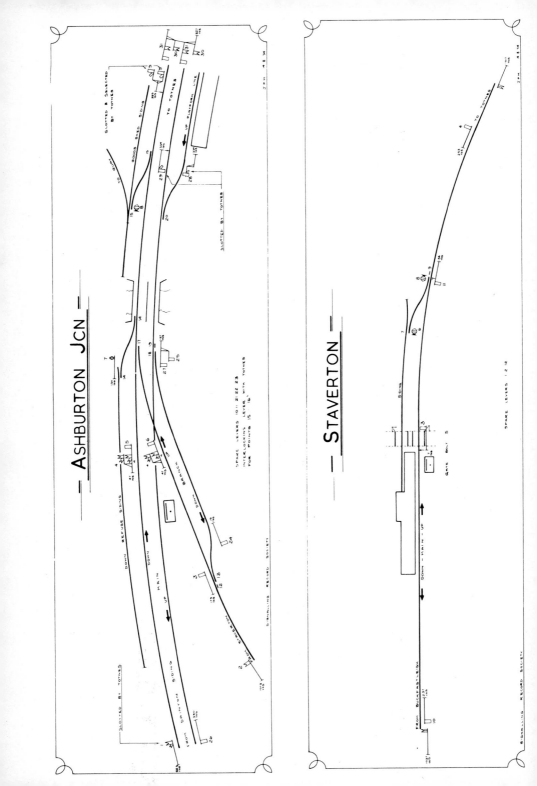

— ASHBURTON JCN —

— STAVERTON —

SIGNALLING RECORD SOCIETY

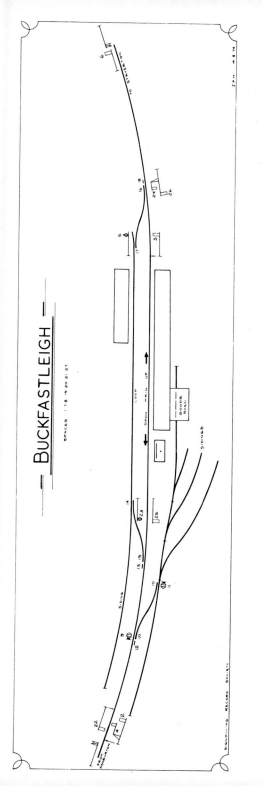

BUCKFASTLEIGH

SPACES 1 7 8 19 20 21 27

SIGNALLING RECORD SOCIETY

TO STAVERTON

TO MAIN UP

LOOP

DOWN MAIN

GOODS SHED

SIDINGS

SIDING

FROM ASHBURTON

135a
Great Western Railway.

Buckfastleigh

TO

Plymouth (G.W.)

CARRIAGE PAID.

No. of Packages

Route via ....

Gt. Western Ry.   Gt. Western Ry.
Ashburton   Ashburton

541   541

To

BUCKFASTLEIGH

THIRD CLASS C.

3d C. fare   3d C.
Buckfastleigh   Buckfastleigh

FOR CONDITIONS SEE BACK (W.)

135a
GREAT WESTERN RAILWAY.

BUCKFASTLEIGH

TO

BRISTOL

CARRIAGE PAID

No. of Packages

Route via ....

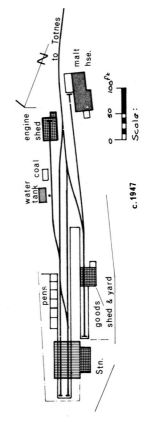

to Totnes

engine
shed

water
tank   coal

malt
hse.

Scale:
0   50   100 ft

pens.

goods
shed & yard

Stn.

c. 1947

ASHBURTON

Opened: 1872

Closed: November 1958

Codings: G.W.R. Sub to NA
B.R. Sub to 83A

Origin: Buckfastleigh, Totnes
South Devon Railway

This former broad gauge depot had stone walls and a slated roof with a central raised vent. The shed measured some 45 ft. x 23 ft. and had a small office adjoining the rear of the shed.

Railway concern, absorbed by G.W.R. in 1897.

Locomotive Allocation 31.12.47:

0—4—2T: 1429

Page from 'An Historical Survey of G.W.R. Engine Sheds' by Oxford Publishing Company

APPENDIX I. MISCELLANEOUS DATA.

MEMORIES OF SOME WHO KNEW THE LINE WELL

Mr. F. Thatcher of Totnes, who was for a time the signal and telegraph officer on the branch, recalls... "Ashburton station was supervised by Stationmaster Dick Dinwiddy, a man of great ambulance administration and first aid knowledge..."

"...In the booking office there was a large variation of tickets that could be purchased, a ferry ticket for 1½d to cross the river Mersey from Birkenhead to Liverpool being amongst the selection!..."

"... In the station yard there was much activity, shunting in and around the goods shed where local tradesmen's goods and grain merchants provided regular commerce..."

"... The walk from Ashburton to Buckfastleigh was pleasant. On the way you could meet Bert Fry the ganger, 'walking his length', a tremendously strong man was Bert, he could throw sleepers about at times, — liked his 'Scrumpy' too! It was a sad day when poor Bert was killed by a passing train..."

"... As one approached Buckfastleigh Quarry, you could hear the thud of the crushing machine and see large lumps of stone reduced to ballast and even gravel. Around the following corner from the quarry was the 'distant' of Buckfastleigh signal box..."

"... the under portion of the signal box at Buckfastleigh was a parking place for signalman Fred Weeks great tandem 'bike, that 'bike must be quite a collectors piece by now! Fred Weeks and his mate, Sad Doidge were signalmen, booking clerks, shunters and general factotums, presided over by Mr. Major, the stationmaster who later went to either Canada or America..."

"... When the goods trains arrived, there was a lot of shunting for there were cattle trains on the branch in those days, plus all the local goods for town delivery and pick up from the goods shed..."

"... After leaving Buckfastleigh, came the walk to Staverton. The river Dart ran alongside the track, making the walk a never ending source of pleasure especially in summer, the variation of flowers, trees and wild life was fantastic! On arrival at Staverton one was sure of a welcome from Arthur Dawe who had given a lifetime of service to the branch. The booking office was something to marvel at, there was a fire place there that Arthur used to black lead polish twice a day. The lino fairly gleamed, everything had a place and everything was in its place. Staverton builders kept the station and yard busy daily with consignments of container traffic for the main line ..."

"...At Staverton the track was maintained by Percy Eagles and his gang and as most of the track was beside the river they knew the river's habits well... one of them, Alf Harvey 'fell' in and had to dry out in front of the hut fire, some reckon he was pulled in!!. Pressing on towards Totnes, one arrived at Napper's Crossing where one could, on pretence of maintaining the block telegraph, stop for a cup of tea and a piece of cake. The Nappers were a railway family, one son was a signalman at Rattery on the main line nearby..."

"... A more serious aspect of working on the branch was the stabling of Royal Trains between Totnes and Staverton Crossing whilst their Majesties carried out occasional West country functions. I was responsible for the telephone communication from the trains site to Totnes station where switching arrangements joined the phones to main line circuits..."

"...Bill Cartwright and Dick Marks must have crossed the river Dart thousands of times with their little push and pull train, but time decreed that it eventually had to go..."

"...Another doomed line at Totnes was the Quay line. This was a line that carried timber to Reeves and cyder to Symmonds, down by the steamer quay. The trucks were shunted as far as the crossing on the plains then Bill Phillips would hitch up his great horse to them. He would then stand by the gateless crossing with a red flag holding up the traffic as the horse would haul its load down to the quayside. Following Bill Phillips place came George Luscombe to look after the horse in later days but all have now gone the tracks, the horse and the traffic..."

Mr. J. Anning of Saltash Cornwall, recalls...."My most vivid recollections of the Buckfastleigh to Ashburton part of the line were, as an Ashburton Grammar Schoolboy in 1929. I used to travel with my school friends between these two towns just after 8.00 a.m. mornings and returning afternoons at 4.00 p.m. after school closed. I remember well the enthusiastic greeting we all gave to the little trains arrival from Totnes, and how we regarded the little tank engine sandwiched as it was, between the two long coaches — as being a machine of super strength to handle such a load!

In the 1920s, the line was of great importance to the residents of Ashburton, Buckfastleigh, Staverton and for many other of the more outlying areas, because it was for them the quickest and most convenient link with the main line. Moreover, as it ran close to the river Dart for much of its distance, it passed through some of the most picturesque scenery in Devon. Fortunately the part of the line from Buckfastleigh to Totnes still remains, owned by the Dart Valley Co, who run seasonal services on it.

Now, whenever I choose to make a trip over this part of the line — I am again the exuberant schoolboy — awaiting the first sighting of the engine into view, dwarfed by its coaches, just as years gone by. Who knows, probably the same coaches which carried my school friends and I daily for so many years still run today."

Mr. L. Littleton of Bridgetown, Totnes, recalls.... "Ashburton was a busy little station, having four cattle fair days per year. March and

November fairs were the biggest, up to ninety wagons of cattle being loaded away to various parts of the country. Ponies from the slopes of Dartmoor were also sent away in large numbers once a year.

It was also busy in the woollen trade, large quantities of wool were received from overseas for the woollen mills. Umber, which was mined just outside Ashburton, was also sent away..."

"...Coal, animal feeding stuffs and barley for malting were constant arrivals by freight train. Ashburton station served the outlying districts by a county lorry service, conveying parcels, goods and cattle foods to Widecombe, Buckland and the like, which could be a nightmare during the winter weather with solid rubber tyres on the wheels of the lorries..."

"...Passenger traffic was never very brisk, except for the workmans train for Staverton and the children going to school at Totnes. An unusual method of shunting at Ashburton was with the use of a wire tow rope, which was attached to the engine on one line and the other end being attached to the goods wagon on the opposite line!..."

"...During very heavy rain, Ashburton suffered from flooding. On one occasion the water was almost up to platform level and an old manual pump was used to pump out the flooded houses and gas works..."

"...Buckfastleigh however, was a much busier station, with the woollen mills of Buckfast, the paper mill and of course Buckfast Abbey traffic..."

"...Large quantities of coal, wool and wood pulp arrived by freight trains daily for these mills. Outgoing traffic was the finished products such as carpets, blankets and rugs etc.,..."

"... Wine also arrived for Buckfast Abbey where it had various herbs added to it and was converted to 'Tonic Wine', this was then despatched to London..."

"...Staverton station, although much smaller was busy for its size with cyder apples coming in and cyder and flowers being sent away during their respective seasons to all parts of the country, the latter mainly snowdrops and primroses to Covent Garden..."

"... Staverton Builders were well served from the station with large quantities of timber coming in and container loads of office furniture being sent away. Salmon caught in the Dart were also sent from here by various fishermen to their friends..."

These memories were of my days as a porter at Ashburton during the years 1928 to 1933, and later as a signalman at Staverton. It was during this time also that the little church at Buckland — in the — Moor had its bells removed for recasting. On their return, it was my job, as acting motor driver, to deliver them back to the church through the tiny winding lanes..."

2nd · SINGLE   SINGLE · 2nd
Ashburton to
Ashburton   Ashburton
Staverton   Staverton
STAVERTON
(W)   1/2   FARE   1/2   (W)
2067   2067

THE DART VALLEY IN MODEL FORM

IT is now some twenty years since I first visited the Ashburton branch—and straightway fell under its spell. It is, in many ways, the epitome of the country branch, though not strictly speaking a typical feeder line. To take but one point, there is no signal box at the terminus, though there is a magnificent timber train hall of Brunelian design.

As it happens, Ashburton, with only six points, is easily modelled and as a result has been reproduced, to my certain knowledge, three times, and probably on many more occasions of which I know nothing. Indeed, I have done quite a lot towards this end. But, although Ashburton is remarkably easy to model, it is not in itself wholly satisfying—it is too simple. Moreover, I do feel that to concentrate on the terminus is rather like going to a first-class restaurant and stopping at the hors-d'oeuvre.

In the October-November 1950 issue I published a plan which included Buckfastleigh, the largest and most important station on the line. This occupied a room roughly 9ft. x 8ft., terminating in a fiddle yard behind a lower-relief Ashburton. This month I give a more elaborate treatment in a room 12ft. x 9ft. which incorporates Staverton as well, and does include almost every important structure on the line.

There has had to be a lot of compression: this is inevitable. Part of this has been achieved by cutting out everything between the centre of the A38 tunnel at Ashburton to just before the A384 overbridge before Buckfastleigh. There is a near 90° curve in the Buckfastleigh approach, but between Buckfastleigh and Staverton the principal civil engineering structures are present. There are, of course, both the Dart bridges; these are, I think, an absolute "must" for their inherent grace. The main scenic work is at Staverton, where we have a modelled stretch of the Dart, including one of the lovely narrow stone bridges.

Construction would begin from the loops upwards, and as soon as Buckfastleigh is laid out running can commence. Ashburton could come along at a later date. It will be noted that I have put a backscene along one side of the Ashburton baseboard, this is because the buildings here do form a natural backing and would make a nice piece of modelling. At the start I suggest a cut off backscene behind Buckfastleigh. But it is possible to model Buckfast village in perspective over the Totnes loop; this would enable you to include the towers of Buckfast Abbey which are just visible from the end of the station.

If there were another 9in. of length, I would love to model the Dart behind the line from Buckfastleigh to Staverton; this would enable the full representation of the delightful bridge on the A384 crossing rail and river.

I hope that this plan will, for once and all, completely sink the idea that a branch line is ideally suited for a small area. To model a branch properly, whether it is a prototype, or a free-lance affair drawing inspiration from reality, you need a lot of room because the character of a country branch lies in its being a part and parcel of the countryside—and to model this effectively you need room.

Incidentally, I have deliberately moved a cafe a little way along the Dart, because it is a very pretty building and just cries out to be modelled.

I have only been able to sketch in a few of the salient scenic effects, to copy the line thoroughly you would need to make a personal survey. The line is being preserved; all you need do is to spend your holiday this year at Ashburton or Buckfastleigh.

This is, essentially, a scenic model, and therefore I have implicitly ignored N, on the face of it the most suitable gauge. The point is that in OO one can get kits for the locos and rolling stock, thus eliminating much of the mechanical modelling. The amount of equipment needed is small, so it would be possible for a fairly determined individual to model the line in N, though as, in my experience, few first-class scenic modellers are really happy with loco construction, it would be best to use a couple of the small 0-6-0 tanks until one could get the correct G.W.R. locos built to order.

The illustrations show the line as it was before the 1930's and were supplied by the Dart Valley Railway Association. Anyone who knows how it is today will realise that, structurally, there is little more than superficial difference.

Railway Modeller February 1968

144

Plan of the month

Dart Valley

by C. J. Freezer

Each square on plan equals 21in. in O gauge, 12in. in OO gauge, 9in. in TT gauge, and 6in. in N gauge.

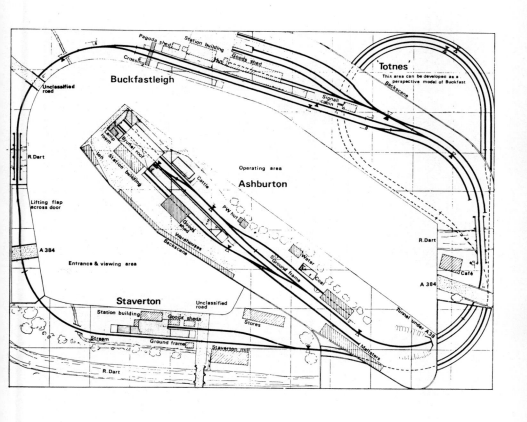

Buckfastleigh

Totnes
This area can be developed as a perspective model of Buckfast

Unclassified road

R.Dart

Lifting flap across door

A 384

Entrance & viewing area

Pagoda shed
Station building
Crossing
Goods shed
Signall cabin

Lamp room
Brunel roof
Station building
Cattle
Goods shed
Warehouses
Backscene

Operating area

Ashburton

P.W hut

Ground frame
Water
coal
R.Dart
A 384
Café

Staverton
Station building
Goods sheds
Stores
Stream
Ground frame
Staverton mill
R.Dart
Unclassified road
Meldon
Tunnel under A 38

Three views for modellers of the now non-existent bridges on the former Ashburton section. (a) The bridge at M.P. 9, viewed from Ashburton end. (b) The same bridge viewed from Buckfastleigh end. (c) The Totnes road bridge north of Buckfastleigh.

R. C. Sambourne

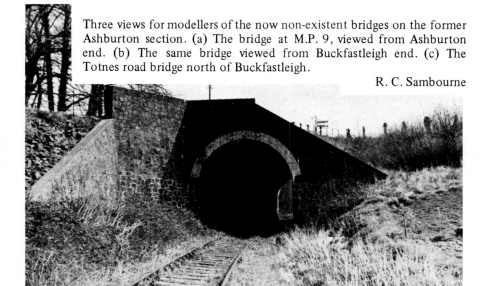

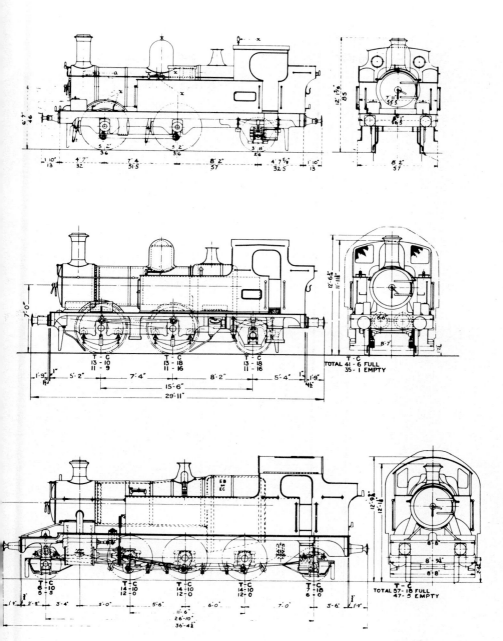

147

Scenes from the Ashburton and Totnes Quay Lines Today.

The outside has altered comparatively little.   A.R.K.

Ashburton station building being used as a garage during December 1975. The trackbed level is utilized as motor inspection pits.

A.R.K.

Ashburton station awaiting its fate during 1972. The track has gone and the new bypass construction has already severed it from the rest of the line.

R. C. Sambourne

View of Ashburton station site as it exists today. The trackbed can just be seen in the foreground together with the engine shed. In the background can be seen the goods shed and the station building.

A.R.K.

A view over the level crossing at Staverton showing the bridge and the road in from Huxhams Cross. Date 26th December 1975.

A.R.K.

View of the roadside entrances to Staverton station. January 1976.

A.R.K.

The new Halt at 'Old Mill Crossing' built by the Dart Valley Railway, pictured on 26th December 1975. A.R.K.

A panoramic view of the new by pass over the trackbed of the Buckfastleigh to Ashburton section. It is pictured from an overbridge and the station can be seen to the right of centre of the picture.

A.R.K.

Remains of the Quay Line existing in 1976:— (a) View of Totnes Plains looking back towards the main line. (Note the weighbridge just this side of the nearest R.H. car.) (b) End of the track just to the left of the bollard in the centre of the picture.

A.R.K.

APPENDIX II. THE DVLR/SDR FROM 1977

The Ashburton Branch, published in early 1977, left the Dart Valley Light Railway firmly in charge at Buckfastleigh and their proposed partners, The Great Western Society, departing to Didcot to form their own independent museum of the GWR. Supporting the work of the commercial venture was the Dart Valley Railway Association, formed to cater for enthusiasts offering voluntary labour and assistance to the operating Company.

A brief synopsis now follows to bring the story up to date, and I would emphasise the word 'brief' as I feel that to list in detail all of the catalogue of events, particularly the very complex buying, shifting, loaning and selling of locomotive power and rolling stock, is well outside the scope of this book.

Beginning where the original book left off, the winter of 1976/77 saw the building of a loop and platform at the southern terminus then known as Totnes Riverside. This work was carried out broadly in line with the proposals included in the report by Mr. Taylor in the DVRA magazine *Bulliver,* as extracted earlier in this book (see pages 90/91), and was achieved with the help of the Job Creation Scheme set up by the Government.

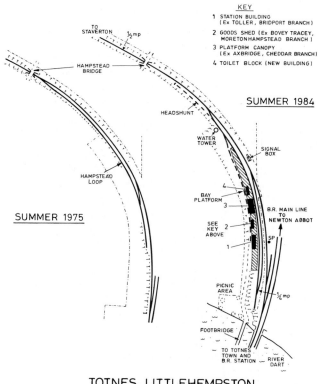

KEY

1 STATION BUILDING
  (Ex TOLLER, BRIDPORT BRANCH)

2 GOODS SHED (Ex BOVEY TRACEY,
  MORETONHAMPSTEAD BRANCH)

3 PLATFORM CANOPY
  (Ex AXBRIDGE, CHEDDAR BRANCH)

4 TOILET BLOCK (NEW BUILDING)

TO STAVERTON
½ mp
HAMPSTEAD BRIDGE

SUMMER 1984

HEADSHUNT
WATER TOWER
SIGNAL BOX
HAMPSTEAD LOOP
BAY PLATFORM
B.R. MAIN LINE TO NEWTON ABBOT
SEE KEY ABOVE

SUMMER 1975

SP
PICNIC AREA
¼ mp

FOOTBRIDGE

TO TOTNES TOWN AND B.R. STATION
RIVER DART

TOTNES LITTLEHEMPSTON
(Formerly Totnes Riverside)

153

The author's wife and grandson, together with the crossing-keeper, watch the last down train of the day negotiate the level crossing at Staverton on 24th October, 1994. The SDR Association members' GW messing/sleeping coach can be seen in the siding in the background to the left.

(A. R. Kingdom)

During 1977 an S & T gang was formed to restore semaphore signalling on the branch, and October of that year saw a fund launched to cross the River Dart at Totnes with a footbridge.

Early in 1978 the footings were laid for a new Buckfastleigh South signal-box, and by Easter a new footbridge, ex Keynsham, had been erected across the track here. Meanwhile, a new building, incorporating a cafe and bookshop, was under construction and scheduled for opening in 1979, and during the Spring of that year the museum at Buckfastleigh, which houses the LSWR Beatie Well tank on loan from the National Railway Museum, was opened.

Over the winter of 1979/80 the new workshop building was completed, prior to becoming occupied on 1st February 1980, and the signal-box at the northern end of the station (the original) was restored and subsequently opened to the public. During the year the 0–4–0 Broad Gauge loco 'Tiny', ex Newton Abbot Station, arrived, also on loan from the NRM.

Following the plan to develop Totnes Riverside, launched by the London & Home Counties Group of the DVRA, the station building from Toller Porocorum arrived at Staverton Yard during the Spring of 1982, while just beforehand, in February, came the development of an idea of DVLR trains running into Totnes BR Station: BR would work out cost and operating details in due course.

The Spring of 1984 heralded the opening of a Tropical Butterfly Farm adjacent to Buckfastleigh Station, and the completion of the structure of the South Box.

Resulting from successful negotiations with BR, the first DVLR train ran into Totnes Station on 2nd April 1985, hauled by 0–6–OPT No 1638. Totnes Riverside was renamed Littlehempston so as to avoid any confusion.

By the summer of 1987 semaphore signals were again in operation at Buckfastleigh, but on BR lines at Totnes the signal-box closed and all semaphore was removed. A year later, by the start of the 1988 season, Buckfastleigh South Box was commissioned, and it was announced that trains would run into Totnes BR on three weekdays only following agreement with BR, but this was subsequently rescinded due to the high costs of the operation.

154

Littlehempston Station building stands as a fine tribute to those who so professionally dismantled it at Toller, on the former Bridport Branch, and reconstructed it here. The exit leads to the new footbridge over the River Dart and into the town of Totnes.   *(W. A. Wright (Sept. 1994))*

On 6th November 1989 Richard Elliott was appointed Volunteer Line Manager, for it was decreed that the railway would be run by volunteers during 1990 to see if they could cope: the DVLR would have closed the line in October 1989 on the grounds that it was no longer financially viable. As a result the last DVLR train ran on 7th October that year.

The South Devon Railway Trust formed as a consequence was granted charitable status in January 1990. In 1991 the line was henceforth called South Devon Railway and although the marketing name, 'Primrose Line', continued, it was allowed to diminish. Meanwhile, in February of that year, David St John Thomas became Association Patron, and on 29th March the first SDRT train ran as a special with the Mayors of Totnes and Buckfastleigh as passengers (the SDRT was granted a 25-year lease on the line and a 2-year lease on the site etc). The Light Railway Order was transferred to the SDRT during Easter 1992.

June and July 1992 saw the working of 'The City of Truro' on the branch, on loan from the NRM. Later in the same year, the South Devon Railway Association severed its connections with the 'Torbay & Dartmouth Railway', and the following December saw the running of the first 'Santa Specials'.

The building of the footbridge over the River Dart and footpath into Totnes finally commenced on 17th May 1993 following financial support from many local and National bodies. It was officially opened by Ian Sproat on 30th September 1993. In July of that same year Buckfastleigh North was re-signalled, and the following October Ian Allan unveiled a plaque — 'Totnes Littlehempston'.

The final item of note has not yet come about but still remains a strong rumour. This concerns the site at Buckfastleigh Station, where it is said that a grand retail development is imminent alongside the station. The results of such development are a matter of pure conjecture, but one can only glean, at this stage, that the SDRT is viewing it with optimism tinged with excitement! (Thanks are due to Mr. W.A.Wright, Commercial Director, SDRT for these notes)

A. R. Kingdom
January 1995

155

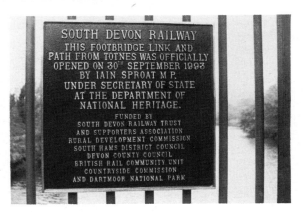

The new SDR footbridge spanning the River Dart and providing access to the town of Totnes from Totnes Littlehempston Station.
Top: The view from the bridge looking towards the station. *(A. R. Kingdom)*
Centre: The bridge viewed looking down river and featuring the former GWR main line bridge behind it. *(A. R. Kingdom)*
Bottom: The commemoration plaque recording the dedication and generosity of its promoters.
(L. Rosier)

156

The last vestiges of the old Totnes Quay Line as photographed by the author in January 1995.

The view eastwards down river. *Top:* The base of the ex GWR 2-Ton loading crane stands silent sentinel to days gone by. Now building works have overtaken the demise of the timberyard and abandoned sidings. *Bottom:* Stubbornly resisting extinction, the last remaining 100 feet of track shows through the encroaching grass, and the bollard hides behind fencing to the left of the flag pole.

Overleaf: The view westwards across the Plains at Totnes showing the old Quay Line Warehouses, now tastefully converted into privately-owned flats.
(Compare these scenes with those of some 20 years ago appearing on page 152)

BIBLIOGRAPHY

A Regional History of the Railways of Great Britain (Vol. 1), D. St John Thomas and C. R. Clinker (Phoenix House Ltd, 1960)

An Historical Survey of Great Western Engine Sheds, E. Lyons, C. Eng., M.I. Structure E. (O.P.C., 1972)

Bulliver – Feb. 1976 (D.V.R.A.)

G. W. Echo's – Autumn 1964 to Winter 1967 (Great Western Society Echo)

G. W. Engines, Names, Numbers & Classes, 1940 to Preservation, B. Whitehurst (O.P.C., 1973)

History of the Great Western Railway, E. T. MacDermot (First pub. 1927: Ian Allan, 1964)

Locomotives of the G.W.R., Parts 2, 3, 5 & 6 (R.C.T.S., 1951–1974)

Rail Trail – Various, Peter Gray (Herald Express)

Railway Modeller – Feb. 1958

Shipping on the River Dart, B. Moseley

Stock Book of the Dart Valley Railway, C. G. Woodford (D.V.R.A.)

The Dart Valley Railway (Ian Allan)

The Dart Valley Railway Story, Hugh Tours (D.V.R.A.)

The Great Western Railway Journal – Autumn 1994 (Wild Swan Publications Ltd)

Track Layout Diagrams of the G.W.R./B.R.(W.R.), R. A. Cooke

THE AUTHOR

There can be few people more well known in local railway 'circles' than Tony Kingdom. Born in Plymouth in 1931, the son of the late Engr. Comdr. Charles M. S. Kingdom, himself a steam engineer with the Royal Navy from 1906 until 1934, Tony became interested in steam at a very early age and still vividly recalls 'interviews' with the driver and fireman at the start and, often again, at the completion of a train journey during the 1930's. Similarly, he also has vivid memories of trainspotting at Plymouth Laira, North Road and Mutley during the war-time years and seeing many locomotives and rolling stock 'foreign' to the area.

With the demise of the steam era in the early 1960's, Tony turned his attentions towards the field of preservation, and the many activities that followed included being Chairman of the South-West Group of the Great Western Society from 1968 until 1972 and a founder member of the Dart Valley Railway Association.

Pressure of work and the responsibilities of a young family ultimately weaned Tony away from preservation work during the early 1970's, but the vacuum was to be immediately filled by him becoming an author of Railway books. This, in turn, subsequently led to the successful publication of no less than seven titles between 1974 and 1982, while in 1990 the lack of a publisher did nothing to prevent the appearance of his eighth book: using the name ARK Publications, he published it himself!

Tony, now retired after a long career in the Post Office Engineering Dept. (now British Telecom), in which he graduated to the position of Engineering Training Manager, Westward District, currently lives in Newton Ferrers with his wife Marjorie. He has two grown-up children, Roger and Nicola, and three young grandchildren, and enjoys gardening, is a keen photographer and, during the summer months, looks forward to boating and caravanning with his wife. In addition, he likes to spend any spare time researching the history and experiences of the Second World War and, looking to the future, hopes to produce further works on Westcountry Railways as well as seeing some more of his out-of-print titles republished.

Other books by A. R. Kingdom:

The Yealmpton Branch	OPC	1974
The Railways of Devon	Bradford Barton	1974
The Great Western at the Turn of the Century	OPC	1976
The Ashburton Branch	OPC	1977
The Princetown Branch	OPC	1979
The Newton Abbot Blitz	OPC	1979
The Turnchapel Branch	OPC	1982
The Plymouth Tavistock and Launceston Railway	ARK Publications	1990
The Bombing of Newton Abbot Station (RAILWAY **ARKIVES** SERIES No. 1)	ARK Publications (Railways)	1991
The Yelverton to Princetown Railway	Forest Publishing (In Assoc. with ARK Publications)	1991

The Author, photographed here with his wife Marjorie